DRY Gardening

Sustainable drought-proof gardening from the soil up

Published in 2007 by Murdoch Books Pty Limited

Murdoch Books Australia
Pier 8/9, 23 Hickson Road, Millers Point NSW 2000
Phone: +61 (0) 2 8220 2000 Fax: +61 (0) 2 8220 2558
www.murdochbooks.com.au

Murdoch Books UK Limited
Erico House, 6th Floor, 93–99 Upper Richmond Road, Putney, London SW15 2TG
Phone: +44 (0) 20 8785 5995 Fax: +44 (0) 20 8785 5985
www.murdochbooks.co.uk

Chief Executive: Juliet Rogers
Publishing Director: Kay Scarlett

Design manager: Vivien Valk
Commissioning editor: Diana Hill
Design concept and design: Alex Frampton
Project manager: Sarah Baker
Editor: Janine Flew
Photo management: Amanda McKittrick
Production: Monique Layt

A catalogue record for this book is available from the British Library.
ISBN 978 174045 9662

Colour separation by Splitting Image Pty Ltd.
Printed by 1010 Printing International Limited in 2007. PRINTED IN CHINA.

DRY Gardening

Sustainable drought-proof gardening from the soil up

Jonathan Garner MAIH

and

Sarah Baker

MURDOCH BOOKS

Contents

Introduction

Think about this. At some time in your life, you've had a relationship with a plant. It could be as simple as climbing a big tree when you were a child or growing alfalfa sprouts on your kitchen windowsill, or it could be a lifelong relationship with the plants in your garden.

For me, gardening is both my vocation and a vacation. For you, it might be a source of organic food, an opportunity to be creative and to interact with nature, or a sanctuary for both physical and mental exercise, making it a great way to relieve stress.

So I've covered some of the reasons *why* we garden. *How* we garden has a significant effect on not just our own environment but also that of many others. We're on this planet as guests of mother nature, so we should behave accordingly.

Here's a ripper example. If I were to tip a litre (2 pt) of motor oil into the drain during a heavy storm, it would end up coating 0.8 hectares (2 acres) of sea water with a thin slick of oil. Not that you would deliberately tip a litre of oil in the drain, but what about the millions of cars with oil leaks? What will their collective contribution, washed down stormwater drains, do to lakes, rivers and wetlands? It's like walking into someone's home with a wee bit of mud on your shoe. It's thoughtless of you not to check your shoes at the door. Lucky it was only you who stained the carpet.

As earth's current custodians, we have failed to respect and value the foundations of a healthy existence — clean air, clean water and wholesome food. If we alter our current behaviour of consuming excessively and producing wastes, we could repair much of the damage that's been done. We would also be remembered as the generation that revived the practice of taking responsibility for our own actions!

How to be a smart gardener

Plants don't ask for much. To grow, all they need is the right proportions of four basic things — sunlight, water, air and nutrients. They are provided with three of these needs via the soil, making it the single most important factor in your garden.

Over the course of a few seasons, this book will change the way you approach gardening by helping you to develop an intimate understanding of the true keeper and master of your garden — the soil. You'll come to understand the natural processes that are constantly occurring and the importance of continual soil improvement using local and natural materials.

A complete understanding of what soil type you're working with, as well as what's going on in the soil and what to put in it, is the foundation of smart,

LEFT Native to southern Europe, this globe artichoke flower bud (*Cynara cardunculus*) will be ready to bloom within five days.

OPPOSITE The majestic pride of Madeira (*Echium candicans*) likes full sun and low humidity.

water-efficient gardening. Learning *about* soil is much easier while you're working *with* soil.

While you're reading this book, wander outside and put what you have learnt into action. Treat it as your instruction manual for smart gardening. It will show you how to improve water efficiencies in your garden and at the same time become less reliant on chemicals for treating pests and diseases, discard synthetic fertilisers as virtually unnecessary and reduce the amount of work you have to do. It will also reduce greenhouse emissions and save you a fair wad of cash.

The principal concept behind water-efficient or 'smart' gardening isn't difficult at all. It's simply a matter of including yourself in the processes of nature. The first step is to change your philosophy. You need to start looking at farming or gardening the soil, not the plants. Healthy plants are a by-product of a healthy soil.

Applying smart gardening principles to the way you garden will:

- reduce your water consumption;
- reduce greenhouse gas emissions;
- save you time and money;
- reduce your reliance on toxic chemicals and unnecessary fertilisers; and
- save your local waterways from pollutants in stormwater.

A water-efficient garden

Water-efficient gardening doesn't necessarily mean locating alternative water supplies or going to the expense of installing an irrigation system. It means making use of the resources you have on hand and using them appropriately, when necessary. We all need to change our philosophy when it comes to irrigation, and regard it as supplementary, not necessary.

Water is one of the vital natural resources for all life on earth. Every single organism on the planet needs water. Without it, we cannot grow food; without food, we have famine. The availability and quality of water have always played important parts in determining not only where people can live, but also their quality of life. Water must be regarded as a finite resource.

About 40 per cent of the world's population lives in regions that directly compete for shared water resources. In China, where more than 300 cities are already short of water, these shortages are intensifying. All over the world, water shortages are reflected in the per capita decline in irrigation used for food production over the past 20 years. Water resources, critical for irrigation, are under great stress as overpopulated cities withdraw more water from rivers, lakes and aquifers every year. A major threat to maintaining future water supplies is the continuing over-draft of surface and groundwater resources.

Land degradation and water shortages are constantly occurring and increasing. Throughout the world, deserts are growing, and life-sustaining and food-producing topsoils are eroding into river systems, blowing away into the sea or crusting up with salt.

Remember the slogan 'Think globally, act locally'? You will be surprised how your conscious efforts at reducing your garden's water and non-renewable resource requirements will influence your overall lifestyle. And you'll find that your kin, peers and neighbours will be subtly influenced to gradually consume less. It's not preaching, it's leading by example. Why not think about it this way: while you're cleaning up your corner of the world, I'm cleaning up mine.

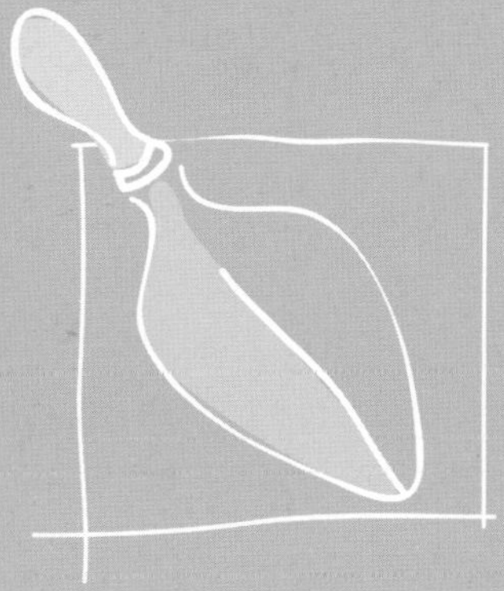

1

All about soil

All about soil

Healthy, flourishing plants are the by-product of a healthy, flourishing soil.

Whether you're embarking on creating a new garden or the custodian of an established one, the same rules of give and take apply. During my apprenticeship, I was taught to look beyond the green stuff above the ground and focus on the brown stuff beneath. As every successful gardener knows, gardening is easy when the soil beneath is in peak condition.

The keys to drought-proofing a soil are these: a crumbly, well drained, biologically active soil with 7–10 cm (3–4 in) of slowly decaying mulch.

The foundation of life

The secret is to feed the soil. Next time you're gardening, feed the soil so that next month the soil will feed your plants. By simply refocusing your energies and changing your attitude towards your garden, you'll reap rewards beyond your wildest dreams. You'll:

- spend less time and money working on your garden;
- need fewer chemicals to protect it;
- reduce the amount of water you use;
- reduce pollutants such as greenhouse gases and nutrient and chemical runoff; and
- increase stormwater infiltration.

And consider the other benefits of working *with* rather than *in* your garden. The health and wellbeing of you and your family will improve and, like me, you'll have more time to spend with your family *in* the garden.

Hopefully, you'll notice that I don't use the word 'dirt' in this book. The soil beneath us is a main player in our planet's ability to sustain life. This irreplaceable resource is here for us to use and nurture, not exploit. For most people who work with the soil, the word 'dirt' is taken as an insult. So never treat soil like dirt!

The components of soil

There's some hard work ahead of you, but once you've prepared the soil properly, you won't have to do it again. There is light at the end of the tunnel and it's not an oncoming train!

Take a look outside. Hopefully, you'll see a plant growing in the soil.

Soil has five main components:

1. mineral particles, the bits that were never alive (rock and mineral fragments);
2. organic matter, the remains of once living organisms or the refuse from living organisms;
3. living organisms, which range in size from tiny microbes up to ground-dwelling mammals;
4. water, the element of life in which nutrients for plants are dissolved, becoming available for absorption; and
5. air, which fills the spaces between the solid particles that are not filled with water.

How the proportions of these five components vary creates the differences we see, feel and smell in soils. Plants aren't that demanding. All they want is a particular balance of water, air and nutrients. When these three aren't in balance for a particular species, it may suffer drought from too much air in the soil or waterlogging from too much water. It may also suffer

PREVIOUS SPREAD Plants like lavender and roses all thrive in a Mediterranean climate and look great in a formal garden.

OPPOSITE The backbone of every beautiful garden is a thriving, healthy soil.

drought and suffocation from no water and no air. This heinous situation is commonly known as compaction. It's like wearing an outfit that's obviously far too small for you. We'll talk more about compaction later (see page 30).

Many professionally landscaped gardens seem to be full of lush, vigorous and healthy plants. But if you look closely, you'll see that most, if not all, competing vegetation has been removed and a generous layer of a soil similar in consistency to potting compost added. No doubt the soil has been overly boosted with liberal amounts of compost and synthetic fertiliser, and doused with water daily. The current popular term for landscape planting is 'installation'.

The roots of the new plants grow eagerly through the soil-blend top-dressing without bothering to burrow down into the native soils. Why would they? Everything they need is put right in front of them. Much like spoilt children, these plants won't cope with the possible hard times ahead. Unless you constantly replenish the organic matter, the soil will lose its goodness and, come the day when the irrigation system malfunctions, it's 'Goodnight, Gracie' for your garden.

The concept of 'installing' a garden is short-sighted and profit driven. We won't be discussing 'landscape installations'; we'll be learning about 'garden building'.

Journey into soil

Let's get down to basics, and discover the components of soil.

In each tiny film of water surrounding a soil particle, there are zillions of living beings doing their thing. Some of these tiny organisms are animals, catching the algae and bacteria and eating them. There are also particles of compost that are so decomposed you can't tell what they once were. That means the compost has reached the humus stage. Humus is open and porous and sucks up water like a sponge. Millions of organisms are busy digesting the compost's organic compounds, releasing their waste products into the water. In turn, even smaller organisms work on these products, forming acids that speed up decomposition.

Some creatures, called autotrophs, convert naturally occurring compounds and chemicals into food for themselves, and sometimes they secrete enzymes that help them break down the compounds so they can digest them. Heterotrophs eat the autotrophs, or their waste products. These creatures form the base of the food pyramid, so all life depends on them.

Humus

This is the life force of the soil. It looks like rich, fertile compost but it's a complex substance — so complex, in fact, that scientists don't understand everything about it yet. Humus is the end product of plant material that has broken down, either naturally in the soil or in a compost pile. It helps the soil to retain moisture and nutrients around the roots of plants, and aids in the formation of good soil structure (see page 23).

One of the attributes of humus is that it feels and smells good.

Throughout the soil, you'll find symbiotic relationships, where organisms live in a state of mutual co-operation, depending on each other for survival. For example, a plant root might be inhabited by small fungi called mycorrhizae. These eat the sugars released by the root and at the same time help the root to absorb mineral nutrients from the soil.

Humankind still has much to learn about these amazing organisms. Less than a decade ago, scientists discovered that mycorrhizae play a vital role in binding soil particles together. They do this by excreting glomalin. This magic stuff has the ability to store between 30 and 40 per cent of its own weight in carbon, thus reducing the amount of carbon released to the atmosphere. That means that 1 kg (2.2 lb) of glomalin-enriched soil can hold and store up to 400 g (14 oz) of carbon dioxide. The root-like threads of mycorrhizae, known as hyphae, act like conduits, carrying water and nutrients to the roots of plants. The network of hyphae increases the plant's access to nutrients and water by several hundred per cent! You heard it here first!

The role of water

I won't go into too much scientific detail, but you do need to know that this sort of chemical exchange happens only when there is sufficient water to carry the electrical charge between the soil and the root. So there you go, water is like a conduit in the soil. When it's not around, the population of organisms in the soil decreases, nutrients are no longer dissolved and plants can't access these nutrients.

So what happens? Growth slows down. As the soil continues to become drier, growth will eventually cease, and if things stay like this for too long, the inevitable happens — death.

Of course, there are other, larger creatures in the soil. Earthworms, for instance, are like mobile composters, consuming particles of organic debris and leaving in their wake tunnels and castings. (Castings are earthworm manure, a nutrient-rich form of food for bacteria and other microscopic composters.) The tunnels are then used by tiny organisms, air, water and plant roots, which also absorb the nutrients left by the worms.

Did you know?

One spadeful of soil may contain more than 1000 species — algae, bacteria, viruses, protozoa, fungi and mites. One gram (1/32 oz) of rich soil may contain millions of individual organisms.

The balance of this tiny universe can be upset by changes in the weather, such as extremes of heat or cold or too much or too little water, or by changes in the soil pH, all of which can lead to large-scale die-offs. So soil is a lot more than just dirt. It's a microscopic universe, teeming with life, upon which all other life depends. It's worth remembering that if we have no soil, we have no food, and without food, we die.

Working out your soil type

If you ever listen to gardening segments on the radio, you'll know that some experts will ask callers for their soil type while other 'experts' won't bother. My advice is to tune in to the ones who ask. Why? Because they're using a holistic approach, addressing the cause of the problem, rather than just the symptoms.

'Soil type' is a general term that describes the texture and structure of soil. Soil is composed of organic matter, mineral particles and air spaces. Soil minerals come in three types: sand, silt and clay. Sand is the largest particle. Silt particles are smaller than fine sand but can still be seen by the human eye. Clay particles are microscopic. The relative proportion of these particles determines the soil type. Once you've determined your soil type, you can begin to work out how to improve your soil structure to create a water- and nutrient-efficient soil.

You may come across the terms 'peds' and 'aggregates', which describe the small crumbs of soil you see when you turn the soil over with a spade. Your quest is to keep the soil organisms happy with enough compost and water that they can develop your soil into a range of different shaped and sized peds and aggregates. More on that later.

Two other items you need to determine are the soil depth and the soil profile or horizons. You've probably heard the term 'parent material'. This is the hard stuff down deep, such as shale, bedrock and gravel. Parent material is what the soil was made from thousands, if not millions, of years ago. Fear not! It may take eons to make soil particles, but in less than a year you'll have enough helpers in the soil to help you transform your earth into beautiful loamy soil.

Our quest is to achieve a soil that:

- feels soft and crumbles easily;
- drains well and warms up quickly in the spring;
- does not crust after planting;
- soaks up heavy rains with little runoff;
- stores moisture for drought periods;
- has few clods and no hardpan;
- resists erosion and nutrient loss;
- supports high populations of soil organisms;
- has a rich, earthy smell;
- produces healthy, high-quality plants; and
- has a neutral pH or is slightly acid or slightly alkaline (more on this later — see page 24).

Soil types

Okay, so let's get on with determining your soil type. Your job is to get your spade and your hat (if it's sunny) and collect a few soil samples from around the garden. It won't take long; in fact, put the kettle on and, by the time you're back in the house, you can pour the tea.

The soil in your garden will probably vary from one area to another. For instance, the soil under the eaves next your house might be dry and sandy, while your flower beds are loam. You'll learn a bit more about soil types as you progress through this chapter, but here are the basics.

Sandy soil

This tends to be very light and dries out rapidly because the spaces between particles are relatively large. Water drains through sandy soil very quickly and makes it easy to dig. (The down side is that dissolved nutrients can't be held within a plant's root zone. Instead they leach away into the ground water.) The temperature of sandy soil fluctuates rapidly and, without additives, this type is lousy at storing nutrients.

Sandy soil has a poor structure and is highly susceptible to wind erosion. It also has a coarse texture, making it dry out quickly, which again makes it vulnerable to wind erosion. Generally speaking, if you live in Australia between the seashore and 10 km (6 miles) inland, then you've probably got this stuff.

Silty soil

The dark soil that's attached to rolls of turf is a great example of silty soil. It holds moisture, is slippery when wet, retains nutrients better than sand and doesn't dry out as fast. On steep slopes, however, runoff can reach high speeds, resulting in erosion. If you live on river flats, in low-lying areas or in any district that has experienced floods, then you've probably got this potentially divine soil.

A little bit of advice: silty soil can compact easily, so always avoid working in the garden after heavy rains.

Clay soil

Clay soil can be very heavy. When it's wet, it holds moisture for long periods, becoming easily compacted, which increases the amount of runoff. It then dries hard as a brick, forming a crust on the surface that limits infiltration and further increases runoff. Although it retains nutrients and is very fertile, it's a bugger to dig because it's so heavy and hard and takes longer than other soil types to warm up in the sun. If you live among tall majestic trees with lush undergrowth, perhaps with rolling hilly areas, then you're probably on a clay soil.

Loam soil

Loam soil has the ideal texture, as most plants grow well in it. Typically, it contains 40 per cent silt, 20 per cent clay and 40 per cent sand and organic matter.

Peat soil

This rare soil type has some pros and cons: dark in colour, it's heavy and highly moisture retentive but very acidic, low in nutrients and difficult to work. For centuries it's been harvested for fuel and is now endangered.

Soil tests

Right, we've covered the different types of soil — now here's the bit where you test the soil samples you collected earlier. There are several ways to test your soil and they're all dead easy.

Sausage test

This quick and simple test will provide you with a pretty general idea of what you're working with.

Simply pull back the mulch, dig down a few centimetres and grab a handful of moist soil. Make a sausage shape by rolling the soil between the palms of your hands and then place it on a flat surface. Gradually bend the sausage to make a circle or doughnut. If you can make one without any bits cracking or flaking off, the soil has a high clay content. If you only make it halfway and bits flake off the sausage, the soil is predominantly silty. If the sausage falls apart as soon as you start bending it into shape, the soil is mainly sand.

Make a sausage shape first, before you bend it into a doughnut shape.

TESTING SOIL TYPES IN A JAR

1 Sieve each sample of soil into a jar.

2 Add a generous shot of detergent, fill the jar with water and put the lid back on. Shake the jar.

3 Allow the contents of the jar to settle.

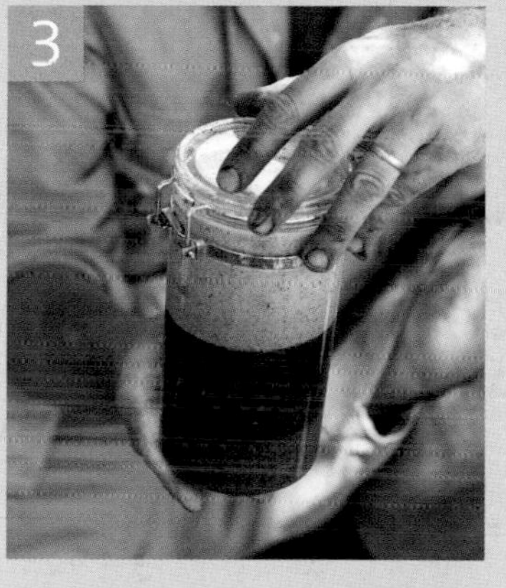

4 In each jar, the bottom layer is sand, then silt, then clay. From left to right: sandy loam, clay loam and landscape blend.

Jar test

Here's another simple test — a classic piece of 'science' from primary school days! It'll give you a clear idea of which constituents of a good soil are under-represented in your patch, be they sands or grits, clays and compost or humus.

1 Grab a clear jar or bottle, and fill it to about one-third of its volume with your garden soil.
2 Fill the jar with water, add a squirt of detergent (a surfactant that will make the particles separate) and shake it vigorously for a minute or so, remembering to keep one hand over the top. (If you have young kids, keep it out of reach, as the temptation to play with this brown muddy stuff will be very great.)
3 Place the jar on a level surface and allow the contents to settle.

After a few minutes, the grits and heavier sands in the soil will sink to the bottom of the jar, while the finer silts and clays will take a few days to settle. The chunkier bits of organic matter (that is, compost) will float on the surface of the water, while the very fine bits that give the water a cloudy or turbid appearance will settle last or possibly stay suspended for many weeks.

These very fine particles are known as the 'colloidal fraction' or 'colloids'. The organic types are humus and the inorganic types are clay. Both are the holy grail of soil biology because they hold elements and compounds used by plants for nutrition. This simple experiment will show you the approximate proportions of sands, silts, clays and organic matter in your soil. After a day or so, it should become apparent which constituents are lacking in your soil.

A water-efficient soil should contain roughly one-third of each of: humus; clays and silts; and sands and grits. A garden is only as good as its soil, and soil improvement is the most effective way to create a better garden.

Soil depth

The soil depth is the distance you can burrow down before you hit an impenetrable layer, such as hard clay, shales or rock. The depth is important because it indicates the amount of soil that's potentially available for plant roots. Also, the deeper the soil, the more water it can hold (although this depends on soil texture and structure too).

If you live in an area with low rainfall — say, 60 cm (2 ft) per annum or less — and your soil is less than 1 m (3 ft) deep, your garden is likely to experience regular drought. And if you want to rely on natural rainfall, you'll have to choose your plants very wisely. Where the annual rainfall is more than 1 m (3 ft), soils less than 1 m (3 ft) deep will help your plants to survive without supplementary watering.

Soil profile

While you're digging down to determine the soil depth, you're inadvertently carrying out another important task — investigating the soil profile. Once again, knowing your soil profile will make it easier to determine what species and container sizes suit your patch.

Taking a soil profile simply means digging a pit in the centre of your garden, about 60 cm (2 ft) deep and wide enough for you to look down and check out the soil. I know it sounds like hard work, but like all the other advice I give you in this book, it will save you time, energy and money in the long run.

As you dig down through the soil horizons, you'll see that the earth changes colour. You should assess these colours along the way, as they indicate important factors, such as the soil's parent material, drainage, aeration, leaching and organic matter content.

RED AND YELLOW COLOURINGS If you have clay, these usually indicate the presence of iron. Red soils are formed from parent materials with a high iron content and are better drained than yellow soils. They can also 'fix' or lock up phosphorus, making it less available to roots, so you may need to use higher rates of fertiliser.

GREY COLOURS AND MOTTLES (red or yellow streaks in a paler colour) in subsoils often indicate periodic waterlogging. In these areas, you might need to improve the drainage.

Soil scientists use soil profiles to read the history of soil formation, but we're just interested in the top two levels — the A horizon and the B horizon.

A horizon

Unless you've just lost your topsoil because you've had a building crew on your plot for months, you should see a dark layer of soil at the top. This is called the topsoil, or what the pedologists (or soil scientists) call the A horizon. The dark colour is due to a residue of humus and carbon, left behind by the decay of perishable plant tissue.

Have a look at how deeply the roots of grass and shallow-rooted weeds have penetrated into the soil. In grasslands, the topsoil might be 60 cm–1 m (2–3 ft) deep, and that's how deeply the grass roots penetrate.

B horizon

Sometimes there is another darker layer beneath the A horizon, known as the Ax horizon, but we're interested in the layer below that — the B horizon, or subsoil. This is the horizon that determines the soil type. It may be the result of weathering of the parent material, which could be mixed in with imported soils.

Soil structure and texture

Now you know the soil's texture, depth and horizons, the final thing you need to consider is the structure.

Did you know?

If your garden area is 100 square metres (120 square yards) and you mix 1 per cent organic matter (300 L/66 gall of compost, or 0.3 cubic metres/11 cubic feet) into the top 30 cm (1 ft) of soil, the soil can store an additional 600 L (132 gall) of water.

Once you've got this sussed, you can plan your soil improvement program and accurately calculate the quantity of materials you'll need.

But remember, whether you have an established garden or you're starting with bare earth, your principle task is to do your best to eliminate anything that hinders the roots from growing as deep as possible. By doing this, you're also improving the soil drainage. Well drained soils hold moisture reserves that are safe from evaporation and evapotranspiration and still available for plants to exploit.

Before we move on, let's clear up any confusion about the difference between soil structure and soil texture.

step by step

TAKING A SOIL PROFILE

1 This soil profile shows a compacted layer. The white layer is brickies' sand and much easier to work than the compacted layer.

2 Beneath the compacted area is topsoil, as subsoils have been dumped on the top and compacted by foot traffic.

If builders have been excavating around your place, they might have left a cutting. Here you can see how the roots don't penetrate the compacted clay subsoil.

Texture refers to the sizes of the individual particles that make up the soil, while structure refers to how these particles may be stuck together to form crumbs or larger pieces. Think of it in architectural terms: if the soil structure is a building, then texture is the collection of building materials.

The structure of your soil may have developed as the result of wetting and drying, burrowing by animals like earthworms and other organisms, the growth of plant roots or the addition of lime. Soils with a reasonable amount of organic matter are much more stable than a soil that contains very little organic matter. The latter is likely to suffer a loss of structure when it becomes wet.

Determining your soil structure

You can determine the structure of your soil by revisiting the profile and horizon hole you dug earlier. If you scrape the side of the hole with a trowel, you can see whether the soil is crumbly or simply a solid mass of individual soil particles.

The amounts of clay and organic matter in a soil play an important role in determining the soil structure. **CLAYS** are made up of minute 'plates' that slide across each other, giving them a very large surface area. Like humus, clays possess a high colloidal fraction. As we

Drainage

This is a bit of a make or break topic. Water is a solvent for nutrients required by plants, and how water moves through the soil affects the availability of those nutrients. There's surface drainage, where water drains quickly across a sloped surface, then there's internal drainage, where water moves vertically downwards.

It's all tied in with the soil texture and structure as well as the soil depth. What you're after is a deep, well structured soil that drains well both horizontally and vertically. Water whips through sandy soil like a dose of salts through your body, while clay soils can hold too much water: as I've said before, each particle of clay has a huge surface area, increasing the

amount of water held by the soil. A soil with a high organic matter content, on the other hand, will hold moisture well but there'll be plenty of space for oxygen. The ideal is to have each pore about half full of water.

Take a stroll around your garden and see if you can spot any boggy, low-lying areas, perhaps at the bottom of a slope, or in a dip. Chances are the soil in this area is saturated. That means that all the pore spaces in the soil are full of water, which leaves no room for oxygen. Roots need oxygen for growth, so if the soil remains saturated for a long period, the roots will die.

Of course, you can fix this problem by various means. Increasing the soil depth and adding organic matter both help improve drainage, but in low-lying areas you're probably looking at some mechanical means to help drain the water away. Here are some options.

Agricultural drains

These are perforated polythene pipes that look like vacuum cleaner hoses. They're laid in a trench with an underlay of geotextile material (see page 73) and crushed gravel or blue metal, which stop fine particles clogging up the holes in the pipe. Dig the trench so that it falls away from the boggy area — you need a gradient of at least 1:60 otherwise the water won't move away.

Swale drains

Swales are shallow trenches that capture runoff to allow the water enough time to soak into the ground. Dig the swale in the direction the water should go and cover it with turf or ground-covering plants to prevent erosion.

Soakaways

A soakaway is an effective way of dealing with a damp spot in the garden. It can also improve the effectiveness of a swale. Just dig a decent-sized hole about 1 m (3 ft) wide and a little over 1 m deep, then fill it with several layers, from bottom to top, in this order:

- stones;
- coarse gravel;
- geotextile material;
- subsoil; and
- topsoil and plantings.

LEFT Installing an agricultural drain.

FAR LEFT Swales have been installed in this grassy bank to reduce runoff and increase infiltration.

discussed earlier, colloids are like microscopic sponges, and they also carry positive electric charges called cations. As the popular saying goes, opposites attract. Plant nutrients, often called anions, are negatively charged. Because of this magnetic attraction between cations and anions, colloids make it easier for plants to access nutrients.

SAND AND SILT do not have any charges, but they are also combined into these aggregates when their surfaces are coated with clay or organic residues. These small aggregates can then form larger aggregates with the help of fungal hyphae, cementing substances from organic matter and plant roots.

In a nutshell, if you have sandy soil, you need to add loads of compost so the soil organisms can convert it into humus. As the humus level increases, so will your soil's ability to store water and nutrients.

Grading soil structure in your garden

You can assess the structure of your soil yourself. Use these tips to guide you.

step by step

TESTING SOIL STABILITY

Test the stability of your soil by adding water to soil aggregates in a small container or saucer.

1 Stable aggregates

2 Semistable aggregates

3 Unstable aggregates

4 Once the aggregates are in water, you can classify them. From top to bottom: stable, semi and unstable.

Did you know?

A single gram ($\frac{1}{32}$ oz) of clay powder can have a total surface area larger than a football field!

STRUCTURELESS SOIL has no aggregates and consists of either individual separate grains, as in sand, or a densely packed mass of particles with few pore spaces, as in clay soils.

WEAKLY DEVELOPED SOIL STRUCTURE has poorly formed aggregates that are hard to distinguish from the rest of the soil.

MODERATELY DEVELOPED SOIL STRUCTURE has mainly well formed aggregates that, when disturbed, will break down to whole and broken aggregates and only a little soil with no aggregates.

STRONGLY DEVELOPED SOIL has soil particles that are almost all in clearly identifiable aggregates.

Soil stability

You can also test the structural stability of soil aggregates by gently lowering a few dry aggregates into a saucer of water and leaving them to sit for half an hour.

1. The aggregates of an unstable soil will disperse into primary particles of soil (the clay particles will make the water look cloudy).
2. If the structure is semi-stable, the aggregates will break down into a flattened pile of very small aggregates but the water will remain fairly clear.
3. A stable aggregate will remain intact.

The benefits of a well structured soil

If the soil simply consisted of a mass of individual particles, the spaces in between would be very small and they'd seriously restrict the movement of air and water, particularly in the heavier soils. For example, a clay soil with no structure would be very similar to the clay used by a potter — a thick, wet, sticky mass that would suffocate your plants in no time at all.

As you discovered at the beginning of this chapter, all sorts and sizes of organisms live in the soil and they can have a considerable influence on soil structure. For example, micro-organisms produce substances that act like glue, helping to bind soil aggregates together, while earthworm tunnels allow air and water to penetrate deep into the soil.

Let's go back to that architectural analogy. Building up good soil structure is like laying solid foundations for a house. These are the benefits of having a well structured soil.

- It will hold large amounts of water as well as dissolved nutrients.
- The aggregates will withstand cultivation and won't 'puddle' when wet or become dusty or set hard when dry.
- The network of pores will ensure adequate drainage and aeration, which are essential for the healthy growth of plant roots.
- It will provide an excellent medium from which seedlings can emerge and through which roots can explore in their search for moisture and nutrients.

If you don't improve the soil structure, the roots of your plants won't be able to grow deep into the soil: poorly structured soil will have 'unstable' aggregates and will be more susceptible to erosion by wind and water. In a heavy textured soil, the aggregates may form large dense clods with few pores.

Improving soil structure

So to improve the structure of your soil, you need to add organic matter and humus.

Humus is an amazing substance. In most situations, adding humus to soil:

- improves the soil's condition;
- helps a porous sandy soil to hold more water; and
- helps a heavy soil to hold less water.

Humus has a greater capacity than clay to hold plant nutrients, preventing them from being leached away in the drainage water.

In a clay soil, adding humus helps to bind the tiny particles or plates together into aggregates, while in a sandy soil, humus coats the soil particles, helping them to hold moisture and nutrients.

step by step

TESTING SOIL PH

Well rotted compost should have a pH of between 5 and 7.

1 You need a pH test kit. Put a small amount of compost onto the board.

2 Add pH dye indicator to the compost and mix it in with a stick.

3 Add barium sulphate and leave for a minute. Compare the colour to the indicator card, which will give you the pH reading.

It may take as long as three to four years to improve a poorly structured soil, because the build-up of organic matter in the soil is a slow process. That's why it's so important to prevent the reduction of organic matter in the first place, instead of restoring it once problems occur.

Providing your soil with a constant supply of decomposable organic materials, adding composts or using green or unaged manures can all help to maintain and improve its structure. Mulching may also protect the structure of the soil surface from rainfall damage. The presence of calcium in the soil may improve structural stability in a few situations (that's why adding lime, which contains calcium, can improve structure).

Soil pH

This is a gardening term that gets tossed around a lot. Basically, it's a way of measuring whether your soil is acid, alkaline or neutral on a scale of 1 to 14. While 7 is neutral, less than 7 is acidic and more than 7 is alkaline. A low acid level in the soil correlates to a pH of 6 to 7. This is sometimes called a sweet soil. Soil with a low pH is called sour, as it can be poorly drained soil with anaerobic decomposition.

pH levels dictate what elements the plant roots have access to. Apart from providing acid-loving plants with the level of acidity they need, achieving a soil with a pH of 6 to 7 will significantly increase your plants' defences against soil diseases and will also greatly reduce your fertilising requirements. When the soil environment is operating at the optimum pH level and there's sufficient composted organic matter, the soil organisms will provide you with all the food your plants need.

Most plants grow best at pH levels of 6.5 to 6.8, because most essential plant nutrients are soluble in this range. The soil acidity varies according to the parent material, the amount of rainfall, the type of plants and your gardening practices. You could have both acid and alkaline soils in your

This pink hydrangea is growing in an alkaline soil.

garden. One immediate indicator is the colour of the blooms of *Hydrangea macrophylla*: in an acid soil they tend towards blue and purple but in an alkaline soil they are shades of pink.

The relationship between plants and the pH level intrigues me greatly. It's one of those rare situations where mother nature provides a 'protected market', so to speak, for the benefit of genetic diversity. There are many plant varieties that can't survive if the soil pH is not in the required range. Azaleas, rhododendrons, heathers (*Calluna* sp.), ericas, Japanese maples (*Acer* sp.) and apple trees (*Malus* sp.) are all acid-loving plants and won't flourish in an alkaline soil. On the other hand, many herbs, rockery plants and most members of the pea family prefer an alkaline soil.

Manipulating the pH level

If your soil is too acid, you can add lime, but the amount you use will depend on the soil type. For example, you'll need to apply more lime to a clay soil compared to a sandy one. But don't overdo it. Follow the manufacturer's instructions about the rate to apply and, as lime dissolves slowly, mix it well into the top 10 cm (4 in) of soil.

step by step

APPLYING LIME

Use lime to adjust the acidity of your soil.

1 Apply lime at a rate of 50 g per square metre (that's a handful per square metre or just under 2 ounces per square yard in the old money).

2 Till it in. We used a mechanical tiller on a large bed.

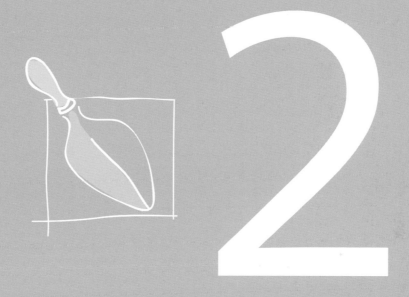

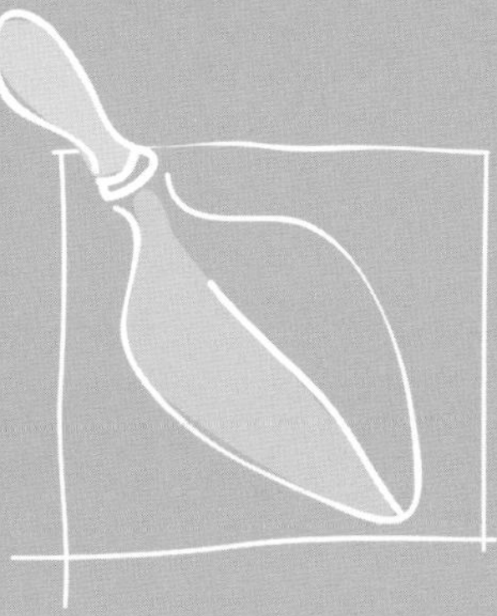

2

Amending the soil

Amending the soil

So now you know everything about the components of a great soil, you can start creating your own — by solving problems and adding soil amendments.

Soil compaction

Soil compaction never happens in the wild, except when herds of migrating mammals are on the move. Soil becomes compacted when some kind of external force pushes soil particles (sand, silt and clay) closer together. In the garden, it can happen when everyone in the household takes a short cut across the lawn instead of using a paved path. Over time, the regular foot traffic slowly crushes and compacts the soil beneath the grass.

But it is possible to fix this problem. You can add wetting agent and perlite, then top-dress with sharp sand. See the technique on page 32.

When a large area of lawn has compacted soil, it's more efficient to hire a turf-corer machine. This self-propelled machine putts along slowly, pushing a series of hollow tubes in and out of the ground. As the coring tubes lift back out of the soil, they remove a plug of soil and turf much the same size as a tube of lipstick. Once you've raked them all up, top-dress the lawn with the sand and zeolite mix specified in the sequence on page 32.

The effects of compaction

When compaction occurs, the soil becomes denser and the soil pores become smaller. The knock-on effect is that the soil's ability to conduct water is reduced. The technical term is 'reduced hydraulic conductivity'. In other words, your garden will never be water efficient while your soil is compacted.

In cultivated soils, this results in:

- poor internal drainage;
- the potential for increased runoff;
- inhibited root development; and
- decreased yields.

PREVIOUS SPREAD You can meet the challenges of exposed coastal gardens by choosing the right plants and paying special attention to the soil's needs.

LEFT One way to avoid compaction under turf is to lay some of this black plastic grid, called grass rings, beneath the turf. It's strong enough to withstand the weight of cars, which makes it ideal for racecourse parking, for example.

OPPOSITE Year-round interest is provided by foliage colour, texture and form. The flowers are a bonus.

FIXING ISOLATED AREAS OF COMPACTED SOIL UNDER LAWN

The soil beneath this lawn of *Zoysia japonica* 'Empire' has become compacted, and the grass is starting to die off.

1 Cast some wetting agent over the affected area, then water it in.

2 Fork the lawn to make holes.

3 Or you could use a tool with a flattened spade-shaped end, like the one I designed.

4 Add perlite — 3–5 L (5–9 pt) per square metre (square yard) — then water it in.

5 Top-dress with sharp sand mixed with zeolite — 5 L (9 pt) each of sand and zeolite per square metre (square yard). Spread it out evenly.

6 Screed to fluff up the grass tips.

If the growing roots can't develop in the subsoil, then the plant becomes stressed and can't make the most of subsoil moisture and nutrients. That's when it becomes vulnerable to the conditions above ground, such as heat and lack of water.

Soil compaction may not affect plants throughout the year; it raises its ugly head during periods of adverse weather conditions, such as excessive heat or cold, prolonged drought and heavy rainfall. Then other stresses, such as insect infestation and disease, capitalise on the plant's weakness.

At this point the uneducated gardener reaches for poison to kill off the pest outbreak. But this sort of intervention interrupts the natural balance in the ecology within the garden, and repairing this damage can take anywhere from a season to a decade to rectify.

Letting your soil become, and remain, compacted is the garden equivalent of Chinese foot-binding! In baking terms, just imagine how hard it would be to burrow through concrete compared to a moist, fluffy cake.

The down side of building works

If you've recently had builders or a cut-price landscaper around your home, then it's highly likely that your soil is suffering from compaction. The current landscape practice of importing and spreading bulk soil with a skid-steer loader may save the contractor time and money but it will cost you dearly. The thousands of dollars' worth of plants you are about to invest in will make your home look pretty for a wee while but, as we discussed earlier (see page 14), the plants' roots will be restricted to the planting holes and the top horizon of the soil. The next heavy rainfall or drought that comes along will teach you an expensive lesson, as the plants will either suffer from wet feet or dry out to the point of permanent wilt.

It's a bummer that during most building developments, the soil is ignored until it's time for the gardeners to move in to make the place look like a home again. By this time the soil is so compacted that the roads department could asphalt it and make a highway through your garden.

TOP A distressed *Viburnum tinus* showing thrip and mite damage. Cut it back hard and wack on a beneficial organism to clean up the pests.

BOTTOM This distressed cycad is suffering from a case of false oleander scale.

Local governments are now beginning to understand what effect regular foot traffic and heavy items placed on the ground under an existing tree canopy have on the tree itself. This compacted root zone essentially starves the soil of oxygen and prevents water penetration. As usual, there's a knock-on effect: if the tree can't receive an adequate supply of water, then it can't absorb any nutrients with the water. What happens next is the slow (or sometimes rapid) decline of this majestic organism.

Cutting corners

Let's take it one step further and examine what goes on in the industry and what it can cost you, the client.

Say you pay a landscape architect or landscape designer to select suitable species and design the layout of your garden. If the designated service provider doesn't have a full understanding of soil mechanics, they might assume that the tree will continue to provide the same 'microclimate' for many years. They'll devise a planting schedule that consists of shade-loving plants, best suited for growing under trees. There might be some kind of barrier around the tree to prevent damage to the trunk and a few metres of the root zone.

Once the builders have gone and the landscaper is up to the planting stage, they'll give some thought to the soil conditions. Quite possibly your project costs have blown out and the landscaper's budget has shrunk. Sadly, the most important task of soil preparation doesn't seem urgent, so it's relegated to the cost-cutting column and that lousy industry method I mentioned earlier is put into action.

Some time down the track, you notice that the tree never looks as happy as it did before the building project was started, and you have to spend two hours of every weekend hand-watering the plants beneath the tree because they wilt as soon as the temperature goes above 27°C (81°F). The tree is now in a state of gradual decline. If it took a long time to grow, it will probably take a long time to die.

One day, the tree naturally dies back enough to expose the shade-loving species planted beneath to hostile conditions, which in turn gradually kill these off too. You then contact the designer and contractor, who might say, 'Well, we can redesign the area.'

You can fix the compaction under the tree (see the box opposite) but of course it's wiser to avoid this scenario in the first place.

Protecting the soil

Here's how. You engage a practising horticulturalist to oversee the building development on a regular basis or, if you can't afford it, you hire one to analyse the site before the builder starts work. They should recommend spreading a 15-cm (6-in) layer of chunky mulch over the soil and properly cordoning off protected trees before installing duckboards to alleviate the compaction caused by vehicle and foot traffic — all before the building work starts.

Once the building job is done, that's when you start fixing the soil properly.

Fixing compaction under trees

The last thing you should do is deeply cultivate the soil beneath a mature tree, as it will tend to fall over or gradually die. The economical and effective solution is to dig a series of trenches radiating out from the trunk. For large trees, this means starting a trench at or beyond the drip line of the tree and trenching towards the trunk. With mature trees, go no closer than 1 m (3 ft) from the trunk, and under no circumstances damage or cut any roots thicker than 2.5 cm (1 in) in diameter. Instead, just gently dig around them.

With newly planted trees, you can dig the trenches right up to the root ball if the roots have not yet grown outwards.

Dig a trench to the width of your spade, then backfill with native soil that you've mixed with organic matter, such as compost. Add some fertiliser if soil tests show low nutrient levels. Within two growing seasons, the root growth can improve by as much as four times the previous rate.

You might need to dig radial trenches for two or three consecutive years, but never dig the same line twice.

Think about how much pressure is forced onto the soil surface when you and the rest of your household repeatedly march over the soil. It amounts to about 3.5 kg per square centimetre (or 8 lb to 3/16 of a square inch). That's like balancing two frozen chickens on top of an AA battery (provided you were clever enough to balance the chooks in the first place).

Fixing compacted soil

If you have compacted soil in your garden, be prepared for some hard labour. The task is to break open the compacted horizon. If the compaction problem is 30 cm (1 ft) deep, then you will probably have to work the soil an extra 15–20 cm (6–8 in) below the problem. That means aerating the soil to a possible depth of 60 cm (2 ft).

Thankfully, there are machines to help with these tasks. If you're blessed with plenty of access, you can't go wrong hiring a mini-excavator and operator. Nowadays you can hire one that's small enough, with care, to fit through openings a little over a metre wide. Trust me, hire the machine. It will do a much better and far cheaper job, especially if you take into account the physio's fees for treating your bad back afterwards. In a smaller area, you can use an electric jackhammer with a clay spade attachment at one end and preferably an apprentice, labourer or backpacker at the other end (you get to supervise).

Clay-based soils are most vulnerable to compaction. I recommend incorporating perlite into the subsoils (20 cm/8 in and deeper) to improve aeration and to avoid re-compaction (see page 46). In the shallower horizons, incorporate composted horticultural bark. It's important to avoid using composted fines or sand as these materials can actually aid in further binding up the soil. Remember, if you mix small amounts of sand into heavy clay soil you're adding the other key ingredient for making house bricks.

step by step

DIGGING TRENCHES AROUND A TREE

You can easily solve the problem of soil compaction under a tree by digging some radial trenches.

1 The soil around this mature tree has become compacted.

2 Dig trenches in a radial pattern from the trunk. Mix horticultural bark into the soil you've dug up and then backfill the trenches.

Tips for minimising compaction

- Never cultivate or walk on wet soil, especially clay-based soils.
- For regular journeys in the same area, use planks or boards on the ground.
- Manage traffic flows: when journeying through your garden, stick to paved areas or use more than one route.
- Mulch heavily with chunky mulch.
- Try to employ a digger machine that has caterpillar tracks rather than skid-steer wheels. It'll be kinder to your soil.
- Aerate turf under and around trees.
- Avoid dumping fill over compacted soil (or you'll end up with interface problems — see page 51).
- Avoid regularly tilling or hoeing the soil.

Premium soil mix.

Soil amendments

To have a water-efficient garden, you need to improve your soil. You can do that by adding soil amendments, which are any materials that will improve its physical properties, such as water retention, drainage and structure. Remember your goal? Creating a better environment for roots so they will explore and grow, taking in enough water and nutrients for the plant above ground to flourish.

Now here's where the hard work comes in: there's no point in plonking the soil amendments on top of the garden or burying them in a hole and covering them with topsoil. You have to work them into the soil. If you don't, you're just perpetuating the problem of poor water rentention, lack of oxygen and poor root growth.

Types of amendment

Basically, there are two main types of soil amendment — organic and inorganic.

Organic amendments

These are the products of anything that was or is alive — compost, grass clippings, straw, manure, worm castings and biosolids. They contribute to the amount of organic matter in the soil and have all the usual benefits — they improve soil aeration and water and nutrient retention, and also provide an energy source for the beneficial organisms that live in the soil, such as bacteria, earthworms and fungi.

Biosolids

These are the byproducts of sewage treatment and may contain heavy metals, pathogens and salt. Choose a Grade 1 biosolid, which has lower levels of heavy metals and no pathogens, but don't use them near crop plants. Some landscape suppliers incorporate biosolids into the soils and compost they sell. There's little to worry about if only a small quantity has been blended with other materials, but I would avoid using the stuff on its own.

Manure

I can see it now. You're driving home after a weekend away and you see a sign that says 'Horse manure'. You

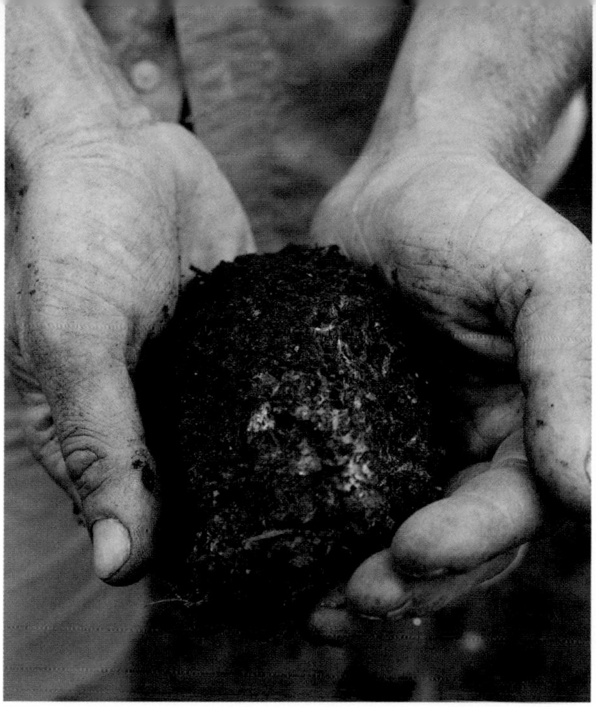

Biosolids.

handy tip

Mulches are put on top of the soil to retain moisture, suppress weeds and moderate soil temperature (see pages 70–4), but, once they have broken down to the point where they can be turned into the soil, they can also be used as soil amendments. (That's another excellent reason for using organic mulches.)

fling some bags in the boot, then whack the manure on your garden the following weekend. But hold it right there. Fresh or green manure contains pathogens as well as high levels of ammonia, so only use aged manure (it should be at least six months old).

If you haven't bought aged manure, you can age it yourself in the compost heap, but please note: most home compost heaps don't get hot enough to kill the pathogens. Before it's safe to use on a vegetable garden, manure must be composted at 54–60°C (130–140°F) for at least two heating cycles. Only use your aged manure on flower beds — in fact, anywhere that doesn't involve food.

To find out more about compost, skip ahead to page 56.

Inorganic amendments

As you would expect, inorganic amendments are either mined or manufactured, and include vermiculite, perlite, zeolite, lime, gypsum and wetting agents.

Vermiculite and perlite

Vermiculite and perlite have one thing in common — a porous structure that enables them to open up heavy soils. They are excellent soil conditioners and, unlike either organic matter or chemical conditioners, they remain practically unchanged for years.

Vermiculite is a product of a type of clay that's heated to 1000°C (1832°F), while perlite is a light, sterile and weed-free volcanic mineral that traps moisture. The surface of each particle of perlite is covered in tiny cavities that hold moisture, while the actual shape of each particle creates air passages in the soil. Perlite also has a neutral pH of 6.5 to 7.5.

Horticultural grade vermiculite and perlite are chemically inert and not readily attacked by soil acids or alkaline solutions. While more expensive than most other materials, they definitely have advantages. They're clean, easy to handle, readily available and, for all practical purposes, sterile when they come out of the bag. They're convenient for seed starting or cutting propagation, for potting soils and for small garden areas.

Wood ash

If you're in the habit of tipping wood ash from the fireplace into your garden, please stop. In concentrated amounts, it plays havoc with your soil pH by raising it to near toxic levels. Wood ash also has a passion for salt, which reciprocates: they cling to each other, making life very difficult for any other organism residing in the area.

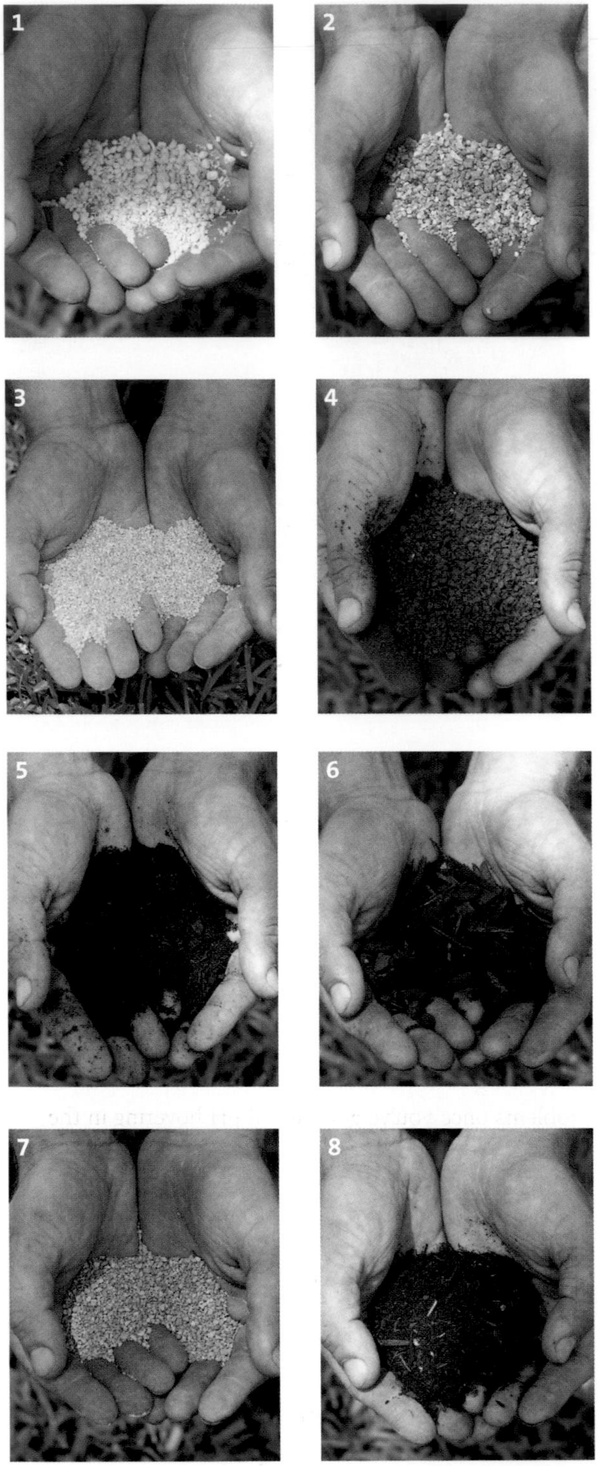

If the material is going to be seen on the soil surface, I prefer vermiculite because it looks more like soil, whereas the white colour of perlite produces a soil mixture that looks less natural. Where the soil is to be used on lawn, the colour doesn't matter so much because the perlite will be hidden by the grass.

Both perlite and vermiculite can be used in amounts up to one-third the total volume of the soil. However, they need not be used as freely as sand. Relatively smaller amounts of either material will result in a noticeable improvement in a soil.

Zeolite

Zeolite is crushed volcanic rock, which holds water and nutrients and gives them back to plants. Use it with turf and sandier soils. It also maximises the use of fertiliser, so you can use less. For example, Australian soils are low in potash, because it usually leaches out, but zeolite holds potash for the plant to use in due course. Just a wee word of warning though: like wood ash, zeolite is attracted to salt and vice versa, so if you're relying on groundwater irrigation with a high salt content — because your bore water has a high salt content, you live close to estuaries or the sea, or your elevation is close to sea level — don't add zeolite to your soil.

Wetting agents

Water has a natural surface tension that allows it to form droplets. Soil-wetters are essentially the same as detergents. They reduce the surface tension of the water and allow it to wet the waxy surface of the soil particles so water can move into the soil through the pores.

SOIL AMENDMENTS

1 Perlite

2 Vermiculite

3 Zeolite

4 Granulated chicken manure

5 Milled cow manure

6 Composted bark

7 Slow-release wetting agent granules

8 Composted fines (on its way to becoming humus)

If you soak water storage crystals in water, they become jelly-like.

Rhododendrons prefer acid soil.

Similar compounds are used in soil conditioners, but when you think about it, if you've prepared your soil properly in the first place, you shouldn't need to add a wetting agent. And they're only useful if the soil surface repels water, such as with a sun-baked soil surface.

Soil-wetting agents belong to a class of chemicals called surfactants. There are different kinds of wetting agents/surfactants, which are used for different purposes. In horticulture, surfactants are used not only to wet the soil but also to allow various products such as herbicides, fungicides and fertilisers to spread over the leaf blades of plants and be more readily absorbed by the leaf tissue. These 'spreaders' are designed to work quickly but don't last long.

Wetting agents and earthworms aren't compatible, as the detergent cuts the worms' protective mucus, which is probably equivalent to humans getting sunburnt.

Soil-wetting agents are available in liquid or granule form. The liquids work very well but are a real pain to mix with water as they make an incredible volume of suds. The granular varieties are usually impregnated into particles like coir (coconut husk), clays or minerals such as zeolite (see opposite).

Lime

The benefits of liming your soil are revealed in the soil pH section (see page 24). You'll be amazed by the increased growth rates and reduced pest and disease problems once you've got the soil pH hovering in the 6.5 to 7.5 range. Just remember that certain plants — such as azaleas and rhododendrons and Australian natives from the east and west coasts — loathe lime because they prefer an acidic soil. On the other hand, Mediterranean plants such as lavender, rosemary and geraniums fancy it.

Mineral rock dust, the giver of life

I know I'm stating the obvious here, but during the last Ice Age and the many before that, glaciers were pretty common. All over the temperate zones on earth, the slow but powerful force of ice rivers slowly ground the pebbles, rocks and shales into microscopic specks of dust.

When things started to warm up again, these specks of dust, or loess, were either carried away by the wind and deposited somewhere else on earth, or were washed down a river onto floodplains and into the fertile silts of riverbeds to form alluvial deposits. The parent material of this dust was a mountain or rock that was pushed up from beneath the earth's crust by either volcanoes or earthquakes.

The soils in Australia, for example, are pathetically poor or weathered. That's because the country hasn't experienced a glacial rock grind for more than a million years. Consequently, the minerals in Australian soils have almost leached away. Without these valuable mineral elements, there is a minimal amount of organism activity in the soil, and without this activity the soil loses structure, and in turn, without soil structure the plants labour to grow.

So what do Australian farmers and gardeners do? They dump tonnes of superphosphate and other synthetic fertilisers into the soil so they can reap an unsustainable harvest. Of course, if the soils are lacking in the essential minerals, the plants will be lacking too. In fact, some plants won't grow at all unless they're constantly fed with all kinds of supplements.

This practice can't go on forever. Hopefully, one day all this will change. We must all learn to nurture our soil so that, in turn, it will provide us with life and sustenance. Sure, Australia has pockets of deluxe soil. These pockets weren't nourished by the powdered glacial granites, however — they were nourished when Earth had a good cough! Earth's phlegm is also known as lava or volcanic ash.

If I'm starting to lose you, then think about this: everything on earth goes in cycles. You may remember the photographs of Mount St Helens, in the US state of Washington, immediately after its side blew out in 1980. Grey ash everywhere. No, not grey ash, but a dose of soil minerals that nature spewed forth to revitalise the

The parent material of mineral rock dust is basalt. Here it is in the form of blue metal (left) and dust (right).

A beautifully clipped formal hedge forms a green wall behind this bed of shrubs and perennials.

precious topsoil. That explosion provided much of the region with a dose of natural minerals in a form that takes hundreds, if not thousands, of years to leach away.

Scientific studies have shown that rock minerals increase yields by as much as two to four times for agriculture and forestry (wood volume), and that a single application has immediate results and long-term effects. Now let's talk forestry for a tick. If a tree holds four times more volume in wood, it's stronger and better to build with, it's healthier and more resistant to disease and, most importantly for this day and age, it's storing four times more carbon!

Interestingly, mineral rock dust — whose parent material is basalt, by the way — suffers the same fate as many other alternative resources. It's simple, it's natural and it's cheap. Glacial moraine or mixtures of single rock types applied to the soil create a sustainable and superior alternative to ultimately harmful chemical fertilisers, pesticides and herbicides. Within silicate rocks there's a broad spectrum of up to 100 minerals and trace elements necessary for the wellbeing of all life and the creation of fertile soils. Hundreds of thousands of tonnes of appropriate rock dust for soil and forest regeneration are stockpiled by the gravel and stone industry. In Australia, the living proof of the benefits of rock minerals are easily seen in the bush adjacent to quarries — the plants are much healthier.

In the home garden, you can broadcast mineral rock dust or granules over the soil before or after planting. If you want to use mineral dust as a fertiliser, remember that it's slow-releasing, so gradually phase out the other fertilisers, otherwise you'll overdo it.

You heard it here first. Tell your mates — it's cheap and it works.

Gardening with heavy clay soils

So you've got a heavy clay or silty soil to prepare. You certainly have your work cut out for you, but take comfort from the fact that gardeners working with sandy soils will have more disappointments in the long run, so don't envy them just because they don't have to dig as much.

Chemicals in soil amendments

I have some serious concerns about the use of chemicals in certain soil amendments.

Water storage crystals

First, these drought proofers don't provide the soil with more water; they merely hold more water within the root zone, extending the period of time between watering sessions and increasing the quantity of water required to rehydrate the soil. So instead of using 100 L (26 gall) of water every week, you'll have to use 200 L (53 gall) every fortnight.

Okay, the labour-saving benefits are there, but what about the present and future environmental costs? Before we discuss the cost to nature, let's call them by their proper name — polyacrylamide (PAMS). I've learnt that PAMS contain small amounts of a very nasty neurotoxin known as acrylamide. According to the World Health Organization (WHO), acrylamide is known to cause cancer in animals, and certain doses of acrylamide are toxic to the nervous system of both animals and humans.

It's interesting to note that since PAMS were introduced to treat drinking water, WHO reports that 'very small' amounts of the toxic parent material acrylamide are now present in the foods we eat.

PAMS eventually break down into allegedly 'inert' products. I'm no rocket scientist, but I do know that virtually every product breaks down to its original ingredients or components. I reckon it's plain commonsense to avoid using chemicals in your garden. After all, you're reading this book — which is all about helping mother nature to do her job.

Chemical fertilisers

For many years, heavy industry has disposed of heavy metals such as arsenic, cadmium, lead and mercury in synthetic fertilisers. The trick is that they add just enough to still comply with the permissible quantities dictated by environmental agencies, then stick a cunningly positioned warning about minimising the use of the product on livestock, pasture and vegetable gardens.

You buy a bag of synthetic fertiliser from a distributing company that uses the industrial by-products as garden fertiliser. Instead of the industrial giant disposing of these hazardous wastes in a responsible (and probably hideously expensive) manner, they sell it to us gardeners so we'll spread a wee bit of their heavy metals over a larger area.

CONDITIONING THE SOIL

You can condition a sandy or clay soil with some coir peat, which is renewable. For distribution rates, check the instructions on the packet.

1 A coir block is made from compressed coconut fibre.

2 Soak the block in a bucket of water. It will swell up to many times its original size. Dig it into your soil.

Remember this golden rule: when the soil is wet enough to stick to your boots, get out of the garden! If you really have to work in the garden during these conditions, lay boards, planks, a thick layer of chunky mulch — in fact anything that will increase the surface area of the load upon the soil. The larger the surface area of pressure upon the wet soil, the less the compacting effect of the load.

And remember this other golden rule: never, ever, cultivate heavy soils during wet conditions.

Incorporating sand

A heavy clay soil needs to be lightened with sand, but if you use less than 50 per cent sand, you're doing more harm than good. Ideally, you should use 60–75 per cent sand by volume of soil. For the average backyard of 100 square metres (120 square yards), dig in about 18 cubic metres (23 cubic yards) of sand. This is uneconomical. It's best to use perlite down deep then add lots of compost in the top 20–30 cm of soil.

Transforming a building site

Let's pretend you just bought your dream home in a new estate or land release. The keys are yours and it's your very first Saturday morning. Full of beans and enthusiasm, you mosey out to the front garden and wave to the neighbours.

You're looking at lots of lovely new homes in a lunar landscape. The property developer and builder scraped off and sold the lovely topsoil long ago. There are some patches of green grass in some homes. Your lunar landscape is approximately 20 m wide x 15 m to the front door (66 x 49 ft), less 55 square metres (66 square yards) of driveway and front path. You have a surface area of 245 square metres (293 square yards) of hard, dry and compacted clay. You've got to turn this bombsite into a landscape asset that will increase the value of your home, greatly improve your general wellbeing and not lower the tone of the street.

Preparing to do it properly

Here's what you're going to do.

- You will do this garden once, with no mistakes, and with minimum water requirements;
- You will make sure your front garden grows and matures so that future generations can drive past and say, 'Wow, did you see that lovely old garden back there!'; and

Add a layer of compost to new beds.

Then thoroughly dig it through.

- You will be the envy of the whole neighbourhood because regardless of whether there are water restrictions or not, you don't need to water twice a week, or even once a week for that matter, because you prepared the soil properly in the first place. You accepted the fact that if you didn't invest the extra money in initial ground preparation, you would have been a mug, just like your neighbours.

Where were we? Oh yes, 245 square metres of hard country and some money set aside, and you're ready to work out your bill of quantities. You've already determined the soil profile, and you've done the soil texture and structure tests. Now you need to open this soil up and keep it open.

The profile test dictates you need to lighten the heavy clay soil to a depth of 40 cm (16 in), which traditionally requires spreading gritty sand to a thickness of 20 cm (8 in), then thoroughly mixing it into the soil to a depth of 40 cm (16 in). You'll need 49 cubic metres (64 cubic yards) of gritty sand. It's going to take a significant sum just to get the sand delivered to your yard and you'll still have to turn the stuff into the soil. Lucky you've got this book — here's a more economical approach to take.

First, locate all utility services and flag the area for safety. If you're not sure where they are, look for a subtle depression line in the ground. They usually run from one of the front corners of your block. The depression you may see in the ground is due to soil settlement after the trench was dug.

Ripping the soil

Next, hire a machine and operator to deep rip the clay with an excavator or backhoe while you carefully pour a 1 L (2 pt) jug of perlite into the void immediately behind the machine ripper. The machine will make a rip as deep as possible and perpendicular to the fall of the land every 1 m (3 ft).

So how much perlite do you need if you're doing 15 runs at 1 m (3 ft) apart? 15 x 20 m = 300 lineal metres (15 x 66 ft = 330 linear yards). So remember you're using 1 L per metre (2 pt per 3 ft) of rip. Therefore you require 300 L (660 pt) of perlite for the deep ripping. This equates to a handful of perlite every 10–15 lineal centimetres (4–6 in). So why don't you buy double and mix it into the top horizon after lunch as well?

Okay, the digger has done the parallel rips in about two and a half hours. Now ask him to do another run of ripping lines, but this time on a diagonal line that's perpendicular to the initial lines. This will really open up the soil.

Spreading the organic matter

While all this has been going on, 20 cubic metres (26 cubic yards) of composted organics from the recycling yard have been delivered. By this stage, the neighbours have stopped peering through their curtains and are actually standing around watching the activity. Each boy under the age of 8 is fixated on every move the digger makes, dreaming that one day he will be a digger operator.

The tip-truck driver was kind enough to dump the organics in three smaller piles along the front boundary so the black and steaming compost will be easier to spread. Fortunately, the ripping takes half the time on the second run. Why? Because when the diagonals intersect with the first set of ripping lines, the earth becomes soft and the job effortless.

You can grow herbs for an ornamental effect as well as for their culinary uses.

As soon as the rippings are done, the operator puts a bucket attachment on the machine, then motors over to the compost piles. If your back is feeling quite sore, you appreciate him scooping up the very light compost and filling your barrow. Once the compost has been spread over the ripped soil, you can stop for lunch.

Cultivating the compost

Straight after lunch, the operator cultivates the compost into the top 25 cm (10 in) of your soil and then runs his bucket back over the tilled earth to break up some of the larger clods. Come 3.30 pm, the job's done and you're feeling pretty chuffed that you actually got a weekend project completed by Saturday afternoon. You can then spend Sunday nursing your aching bones while thumbing through nursery catalogues or doing the final planting schedule. RESULT!

Working on an existing garden

If you've got the same problem but your yard has existing plants, then approach the task like this.

Clearing the area

Clear the area of unwanted vegetation. If there are any particularly precious plants within the improvement area, and you don't want to disturb them, it's OK to work around them, provided that you take care to avoid excessive root damage. If you can, dig the plants out and store them somewhere suitable until you can re-plant them.

Breaking up the soil

Use a garden fork to break up the soil by driving it in and levering it back to lift the soil. You need to loosen at least the top 20 cm (8 in) of the existing soil, and you may want to consider the double-dig technique for deeper improvement (see pages 46–8). There is no need to turn the soil a great deal at this stage, as you'll be doing plenty of that shortly.

Working in the amendments

Once you've broken up the ground, scatter the perlite/vermiculite and/or organic matter over the surface to a depth of 75–100 mm (3–4 in), and then, again

step by step

BREAKING UP COMPACTED SOIL

1 This rock-sized lump of compacted soil is so rammed together that neither water nor roots can penetrate it.

2 Rake perlite over the compacted area.

3 Use a jackhammer through the perlite to break up the soil and distribute the perlite. In a small area you could use a gardening fork, but if the soil is rock hard, that's likely to bend the tines on your fork.

using a fork, turn the soil over, mixing in the added material as you work. Try to break up any clumps of soil with the tines of the fork, so that there are no clumps bigger than about 40–50 mm (1½–2 in). Keep turning the soil until it is reasonably well mixed and there are no obvious patches of all-soil, all-sand or all-humus.

If the soil is 'sumo wrestler' heavy and clods up when wet, I suggest you locate supplies of composted horticultural bark. But please make sure it's composted. This chunkier stuff will ensure the soil clods don't stick together again.

If the soil is very heavy and you're a fan of power tools, then pop down to the tool-hire shop for an electric jackhammer with a clay spade attachment. This is my weapon of choice, as it's easier on my back and gets the job done in half the time.

Once you've opened up the compacted layer of soil properly, use a rotary hoe to break up the large clods while mixing the additives. Two words of warning though: if you've been lazy and haven't addressed the compaction problem, the blades on the rotary hoe will bounce along the compacted layer, making it worse than before. But as you bought this book to learn how to garden efficiently and effectively, you can happily leave scenarios like that to the cowboys.

Double digging

This labour-intensive method of soil preparation provides an excellent rooting zone for plants and is great for developing perennial borders and vegetable patches. It involves removing the topsoil to the depth of a spade, setting the soil aside and then loosening the subsoil another spade's depth. Finally, the topsoil is returned with added amendments, such as compost, manure or fertilisers.

OPPOSITE With a well drained soil, both ornamentals and annuals will self-sow.

step by step

DOUBLE DIGGING

This technique improves the soil quality and brings the soil level up.

1 Jackhammer the soil with a spade fitting to just over the depth of the spade. Remove any bulky bits and separate the clods and rocks.

2 Dig one trench to 20 cm (8 in).

3 Add perlite.

4 Add composted fines to the trench, forking it in and loosening the soil another spade depth before you backfill from the next trench, which you need to dig alongside the first.

Avoid hauling in new layers of soil without mixing them into the existing soil. Distinct layers of soil create barriers through which water will not readily penetrate and roots will not easily grow. Soil interface problems are the most common reasons for turf failure, but we'll chat about that later (see page 51).

If you double dig one patch of heavy clay soil then single dig another, the vegetables and flowers in the double-dug patch will grow twice as fast, have 50 per cent more yield, fewer pests and diseases, and require 25 per cent less water.

The curse of sandy soil

Sandy soil is easy on your back, yet costs a lot in resources. As we learnt in the previous chapter, sandy soils generally drain too fast, so they're unable to hold onto any nutrients long enough for a plant to use them. Organic matter helps to hold onto water and nutrients and, as with clay, it's almost impossible to add too much. A higher ratio of organic material to sand is a good option: the organic matter tends to break down faster because the greater amount of available oxygen and higher soil temperatures increase the rate of drainage.

The waterproof effect

We always hear that sandy soils are well drained and rapidly absorb water, so why is it that when you pour water on very dry, sandy soils, it behaves as though it's been poured onto a waterproof fabric? The water stays in beads and runs off without even attempting to soak in. I'm glad you asked, because I now have the opportunity to drop in another impressive word — hydrophobia.

These conditions can be a trap for gardeners who think they've watered their plants when, in fact, the water has simply rolled to the sides of the pot and out the drainage holes without wetting the soil at all. So 'well watered' pots can often be seriously drought stressed.

These conditions become especially perilous when you're planting out. Do not stick a hydrophobic root ball into the ground without drenching it thoroughly beforehand. Essentially, unless the species you're planting is a bulletproof variety, you're condemning it to certain death. It won't matter how much water you give it after planting, the root ball will never properly rehydrate and the plant will never establish itself. You see, the particles of soil and organic matter become so dry that some products made by your soil organisms become waxy substances and actually repel the water.

Solving the hydrophobia problem

The most effective solution, of course, is prevention. I have a few suggestions.

1 Don't let the sun bake the soil surface: maintain a decent thickness of mulch, which also creates a friendly environment for the helpers in the soil so they can carry on doing what they do best.
2 Slowly moisten the soil over a long period. Showers of rain work perfectly to rehydrate soils.
3 The most effective solution for fixing a hydrophobic pot plant is to dunk the root ball in a big bucket of water and leave it there for about five minutes. This will give the soil particles the chance to get drenched and will also eliminate any ant colonies that may have taken up residence. (Obviously, you should use your judgment and commonsense about which plants won't enjoy this treatment.)
4 When it comes to planting out, I'm a huge fan of giving every plant a swim in the kids' wading pool prior to tucking them into their final residence. Adding a good dose of seaweed extract to the pool is not a bad idea either.
5 Increase the clay contents of the sandy soil by more than 10–15 per cent and virtually eliminate hydrophobia. Use some clay 'soup (see page 50), or spread 10–13 kg (22–29 lb) of clay soil over every square metre (square yard) of sandy soil. Gently tickle the top 10 cm (4 in). The clay will also deliver some trace elements in an organic form.

step by step

FIXING HYDROPHOBIC SOIL

Only use a wetting agent when the soil is hydrophobic and nothing else works.

1 This sandy soil is hydrophobic — it repels water rather than absorbs it. Water just runs over the surface.

2 Wetting agent added to the soil helps the water to soak in.

step by step

MAKING CLAY 'SOUP'

You can condition sandy soil with a clay 'soup'.

1 Here's the sandy soil in my garden that I've been rattling on about.

2 Put some clay sods in a bucket that's half full of water and break them up.

3 When it's the consistency of 'soup', pour it onto the sandy soil. You don't need to dig it in.

6 Your last resort should be to reach for soil-wetting agents, which help to overcome the effects of waxy organic coatings on the surface of the soil and the surface of organic matter, allowing the water to penetrate and be absorbed. Basically they work by making water wetter! (See page 42.)

Amending a sandy soil

About five years ago, we moved close to the beach. Since then, I've managed to transform the grey, lifeless fine sand to a humus-rich and fertile soil. It's still nowhere near where I want it to be, yet I've managed to achieve a garden that requires minimal watering but demands constant supplies of soft mulches. Soft mulches are non-woody organic matters such as straw, sugar cane mulch, lawn clippings, vegetable scraps, lucerne and anything else that rots quickly or is digested rapidly by the Jurassic-sized earthworms that have taken up residence in my garden.

These rapidly decaying mulches provide the soil organisms with plenty to feast on and, in return, provide me with the necessary gluing agents to bind the grey sand particles together and form those peds and aggregates we talked about earlier.

Making clay 'soup'

My impatience with this sandy patch has led me to locate pool builders who are working in districts with clay soils. If you can source a supply of clayey soils, that's the best stuff for transforming your sandy soil. The beauty of clay is its ability to hold nutrients and trace elements. I'm a huge fan of pulverising clay soil in a bucket of water to make clay 'soup', then watering my sandy soil with this brown soup as often as possible. Give it a go, and watch the changes that happen before your very eyes. The sand will start to cling together and the soil's nutrient and water requirements will fall significantly, as will the incidence of pests and diseases. Once again, this practice is all about the quest to form peds and aggregates within the soil.

Sandy soil and growing turf

The benefits of sandy soils are pretty well limited to one thing. They don't suffer from compaction. This makes them ideal for growing turf on, right? Well, sometimes they are. It's important to have the right-sized particles in your sand. The sand in my garden is fine and uniform, which makes it behave a little like clay when it's watered. The water slowly filters in while the air is forced out (which makes it not such a great soil). Each year, however, things improve. Both the soil structure and plant health are improving and, at the same time, I'm using less and less water.

Sandy soils are brilliant for growing turf. Why? Because sand doesn't compact like silt and clay do. People like to walk on turf, and where people walk, the soil compacts. (We gardeners only like compacted soils under our paving and roads.) But if your sandy soil is like mine and consists of uniformly sized particles, it'll lack pore spaces for air. In this case, add screened compost fines, perlite or a sand with larger particles.

Now the pearl of wisdom I'm about to give you is a vital piece of the soil drainage puzzle. It also makes the majority of the landscaping industry look like hapless fools for failing to effectively and efficiently provide the consumer with a lawn that can tolerate foot traffic, shaded areas, reduced irrigation and greatly reduced pests and diseases. The name of this pearl is 'soil interfacing'.

Soil interfacing or layering

If there's only one thing you learn and remember from my rants it should be this: you will never have a water-efficient microclimate or a truly healthy and happy garden if you have a soil interface. The thing that really rubs my rhubarb is the fact that most people who have this trouble actually paid a contractor to provide them with this drainage nightmare.

Interfacing happens when you plant out with a planting soil that is quite different to the backfill soil. But the best example of interfacing happens to be common practice within the landscape industry: mass top-dressing of landscape soil blends over existing soils without mixing the different materials together. This practice creates an instant effect: initially rapid growth yet, in the long term, an unsustainable garden.

The difference in pore spaces and sizes between the two soils makes it difficult for water to filter through the interface zone. Then excess water becomes stuck at this layer, creating waterlogged conditions. When you add the copious amounts of composted organics in the landscape blend, you now have a problem called anaerobic conditions. This ugly situation leads to the soil becoming toxic. The plant will either suffer drought or blow over. The next and final step is the death of your plants and a waste of your hard-earned money.

The simplest way to demonstrate interfacing is to fill your bath tub, then pull the plug out and replace it with a face cloth or some other porous fabric. The fabric acts just like a plug and creates a situation called 'perched water table'.

Laying turf over a soil interface

I reckon this practice takes the cake. The contractor or the do-it-yourselfer has followed the turf supplier's instructions. They've prepared a soil of approximately 15 cm (6 in) of well drained, sandy soil mix, consolidated it and are about to ruin all that hard work by laying carpets of turf that are green on one side and deep brown to black on the other.

This dark-coloured, fertile and very sticky soil is fantastic for cutting and transporting turf, but when it's laid over your well drained sandy soil mix, it creates an interface that easily compacts, holds excessive moisture and prevents water from filtering down into the subsoils.

This problem compounds when it's winter and the soil is in the shade. The damp oxygen-poor silt is concentrated around the turf stolons (or runners) and creates a wonderful environment for rot and other diseases to set in. The best practice is either to get the turf farm to wash the soil from it or remove as much of it as possible yourself before you lay the turf. The next step is to top-dress the laid turf with the same soil you used beneath. It's a harder job but, wow, the results speak for themselves (see pages 114–15). If you need proof, check out how turf is laid on golf courses and playing fields.

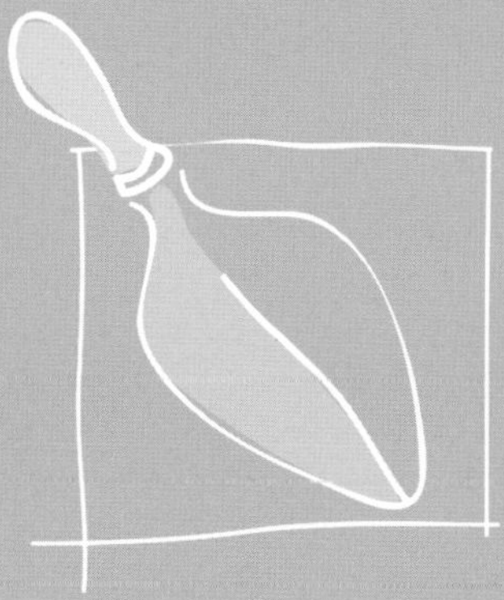

3

Compost and mulch

Compost and mulch

Using compost regularly and continually mulching your garden beds will improve the soil's texture and structure and, most importantly, nourish the foundations of your garden.

Compost

We live in a consumer-driven, throwaway society, where nearly every product we buy comes with lots of packaging. You may be a responsible consumer who carefully separates your recyclable materials before you put the garbage out each week, but maybe you also put out your green waste for the regular council collection. The council will take these materials to a composting yard, where they'll be composted and screened in bulk, then sold back to you as commercial products.

But if you recycle your food scraps and garden waste into your own compost pile, you can reduce your contribution to landfill by as much as 30 per cent. You can also, and here's the good bit, make a fantastic product that will improve the texture and structure of your soil as well as help it retain nutrients and water within the root zones of your plants, so you can do your bit for the environment and benefit your garden at the same time.

You'd have to agree that whenever you read a gardening article, hear gardening advice or read a plant label, the word 'compost' or the term 'well rotted organic matter' is dropped in there somewhere. So you know what it looks like, you know what it feels like and by now you should know what benefits it brings to your soil and plants. Let me introduce you to the art and science of composting.

A potted history of compost

There is evidence that humankind knew about the value of compost thousands of years ago. Both the Talmud and the Bible refer to the uses of rotted manure straw, and famous Elizabethans such as William Shakespeare and Sir Walter Raleigh also mentioned the use of compost in their writings.

Typically, during the ecologically disastrous period of industrialisation, our intelligent yet unwise scientific

PREVIOUS SPREAD In a woodland garden, fallen leaves and plant debris have been left to form a nourishing mulch.

LEFT If the council picks up your green waste, this is where it'll probably end up — in an enormous green waste pile that will be shredded, composted and graded before it's guaranteed pathogen- and weed-free.

OPPOSITE This garden has been carefully designed and planted to look natural and provide privacy.

Squeeze some compost through your fingers and find out how good it feels.

community thought they could outdo mother nature and develop a new 'scientific' method of farming. In 1840, a German chemist, Justus von Liebig, proved that plants can obtain nourishment from certain chemicals in solution; however, he failed to recognise the significance of humus, because it was insoluble in water.

Liebig's discovery turned out to be a shot in the arm to the chemical industry. Naturally, farmers thought it was much easier to buy a bag of fertiliser than to mess around with manure, so they replaced compost with chemical fertilisers. This change in farming practice was nothing short of disastrous. Stop and think for a tick about the effects of eliminating organic matter from soil. It has resulted in:

- increased soil compaction;
- ruined soil structure;
- decreased air movement within the soil (reduced air-filled porosity);
- decreased water movement in the soil (reduced hydraulic conductivity);
- increased nutrient leaching and runoff into waterways, thus polluting drinking water;
- polluted and dying coral reefs, thanks to nutrient runoff;
- eroded precious topsoil, resulting in floods, famine and desertification; and
- excessive irrigation, which has led to dry land salinity and soil acidification.

The list goes on and on. (Note that I have used some 'knock-em-dead/don't-question-my-knowledge' technical terms that are guaranteed to fortify your garden guru status if you utter them at dinner parties.)

So here we have another shining example of the perils of manipulating an ecological system instead of following mother nature's lead.

In my opinion, although Justus von Liebig made some important discoveries that benefited the human race, his blinkered obsession with the 'benefits' of chemicals has created pain and suffering while helping to fatten the wallets of multinational synthetic fertiliser companies.

Howard and Rodale

Fortunately, in the twentieth century, a couple of blokes investigated and experimented with organic farming. In 1943 Sir Albert Howard, a British agronomist, published a book called *An Agriculture Testament*, which was based on nearly 30 years' experience of organic gardening and farming. Now regarded as the modern father of organic gardening and farming, Howard found that the best quality compost was the result of layering and turning a compost pile that consisted of one part manure and three parts plant material.

An American named J J Rodale was another pioneer in organic farming techniques. He introduced composting to American gardeners and established a monthly magazine called *Organic Gardening*.

The benefits of compost

Compost to soil is much like breast milk to babies — it has many wonderful properties that we still don't fully understand. Just like the manufacturers of baby formula, the manufacturers of chemical fertilisers haven't been able to come up with a product that competes with the holistic qualities of the real thing. Science can synthesise and package the essential ingredients for nourishment of most organisms, but it fails to provide the essential blend of amino acids, complex proteins and various enzymes that, when combined by natural processes, become the wholesome foundation of a healthy life.

Here's what compost does for your garden. This fantastic organic product:

- improves the soil structure and texture, porosity and density, creating a better environment for plant roots;
- increases the moisture infiltration and permeability of heavy soils, reducing erosion and runoff;
- improves the soil's water-holding capacity, reducing water loss and leaching in sandy soils;
- supplies a variety of macro- and micro-nutrients;
- may control or suppress certain soil-borne plant pathogens;
- supplies significant quantities of organic matter;
- improves the cation exchange capacity of soils and growing media, thus improving their ability to hold nutrients for plant use (to brush up on this topic, refer to pages 14–15);
- supplies beneficial micro-organisms to soils and growing media;
- encourages worm activity in the soil, providing the garden with fantastic nutrients;
- improves and stabilises soil pH;
- can bind and degrade specific pollutants;
- reduces the amount of waste sent to landfill; and
- actively absorbs or sequesters greenhouse gases.

How composting works

Once you understand how the process works, you'll be able to 'read' what's going on in your pile and make the appropriate adjustments if you run into problems.

Micro- and macro-organisms

Although you have to maintain your compost pile by regularly watering and turning it, the real work is achieved by various types of organisms.

Micro-organisms such as bacteria, fungi and actinomycetes are the chemical composters in your heap: they

A minimalist courtyard garden, designed by Vladimir Sitta.

handy hint

The following materials will attract disease pathogens and vermin, so never add them to your compost pile.

- *anything that's been treated with chemicals*
- *dairy products*
- *diseased plant material*
- *fats, grease and oils*
- *meat*
- *pet manure*
- *salt*
- *weed seeds*

Rich compost, ready to nourish your soil.

change the chemistry of organic wastes. The physical decomposers or macro-organisms — mites, centipedes, snails, millipedes, spiders, slugs, beetles, ants, flies and earthworms — aid in the decomposition process by physically breaking down matter into smaller particles by grinding, chewing, tearing and sucking.

Bacteria

The most important decomposers are aerobic bacteria, which utilise carbon as a source of energy by oxidising organic material, a process that heats up the compost pile pretty quickly. Aerobic bacteria excrete plant nutrients such as nitrogen, phosphorus and magnesium, but they need at least 5 per cent oxygen to survive. Below that level they die, slowing decomposition by up to 90 per cent. Once this happens, anaerobic bacteria take over the pile and produce smelly and sometimes toxic substances.

Depending on the temperature, different types of aerobic bacteria can be active in your compost pile.

PSYCHOPHILIC BACTERIA are active between 13 and 21°C (55 and 70°F). They give off just enough heat to allow mesophilic bacteria to take over.

MESOPHILIC BACTERIA produce acids, carbon dioxide and heat as they do their decomposition work. They in turn die off at 38°C (100°F), to be replaced by thermophilic bacteria.

THERMOPHILIC BACTERIA raise the temperature in the compost pile to between 54 and 71°C (130 and 160°F). You have to keep turning the compost pile and adding new materials, otherwise these bacteria will use up the degradable material and die off, lowering the temperature. Then the mesophilic bacteria become dominant again.

Temperatures above 60°C (140°F) are necessary for killing off pathogens and weed seeds, but as I mentioned in an earlier chapter (page 37), the home compost pile rarely gets that hot.

Come to think of it, this temperature business is a bit tricky. If the temperature rises above 71°C (160°F), the composting material may become sterile and lose its ability to fight disease, but you can fix this easily enough by turning the pile. If you're serious about composting,

If you have the space, it's a good idea to have a separate bin for prunings so they can rot down a bit before you add them to the compost pile.

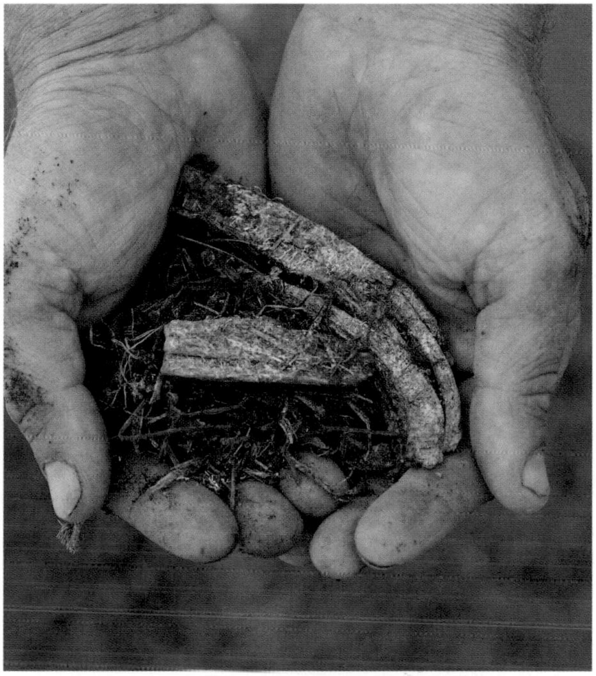

Actinomycetes are bacteria-like fungi that break down wood in compost.

it might be worthwhile buying a compost thermometer from a garden centre, or you could rig up an ordinary thermometer on a long piece of wood or a stick that you can insert into the middle of the pile.

And don't forget to take into account the ambient air temperature. For instance, if you live in a cold climate, in winter you'll need to cover the pile with a tarp to retain the heat (unless you have a compost bin as opposed to a pile — more about types of bins later). In the warmer months, higher temperatures will help to speed up decomposition.

Actinomycetes

Like moulds and fungi, these are another, higher form of recyclers. In the later stages of decomposition, actinomycetes are responsible for decomposing some of the tougher materials in the compost pile — such as wood, starches and proteins — and producing carbon, nitrogen and ammonia.

These primitive plants break down cellulose and lignin, and different types prefer different temperatures. Many actinomycetes produce chemicals that kill nearby bacterial and fungal organisms. One of these is streptomycin, the first effective treatment for tuberculosis.

Macro-organisms

There's a food chain operating in your compost pile — ants feed on a variety of matter, including fungi and other insects, and move minerals around as they work, making the pile richer in phosphorus and potassium.

Meanwhile, millipedes eat soft decaying vegetation while centipedes consume insects and spiders. Other macro-organisms include beetles, snails and slugs, but the most important of all is the earthworm — always the sign of a mature compost heap.

Earthworms digest organic matter and leave behind fertile castings, rich in plant nutrients such as nitrogen, calcium, magnesium and phosphorus. One worm can

Did you know?

Rich in potassium and nitrogen, the leaves of comfrey are good compost boosters. Regularly harvest the outer leaves and add them to your pile.

Harvest the younger leaves of comfrey (*Symphytum officinale*) to mulch tomatoes, capsicum and berry bushes.

produce its own weight in castings each day. (For more info on the wonderful earthworm, see page 15.)

Carbon to nitrogen ratio

In order to maintain a healthy compost pile in the optimum temperature range for decomposition, you need to keep the carbon to nitrogen ratio between 25:1 and 30:1. In other words, you need 25–30 times more carbon (dry plant materials such as leaves and wood chips) than nitrogen (wet and green materials such as fresh grass clippings and food scraps).

If your pile is too high in nitrogen, it will smell of ammonia gas. It may also become too acidic, which is toxic to some micro-organisms.

If you're not sure what sort of materials are suitable for a compost heap, and whether they fall into the nitrogen or carbon category, have a look at the table below. Now bear in mind that even though many of these materials possess the ideal ratio, if there is too much liquid within the material, it will go stinky and slushy.

Types of compost bin

There are several types of prefabricated bin on the market. You can choose from plastic tumblers or bins and wooden boxes. A tumbler produces compost more quickly than a pile, but you have to turn it regularly and when it's full, that can take some effort.

Building a compost bin

If you have the space and some bits of wood left over from a DIY project, I reckon it's easy enough to make your own — even two, each in various stages of

SUITABLE MATERIALS FOR A COMPOST PILE

Carbon-rich materials	Nitrogen-rich materials
Autumn leaves: 60:1	Comfrey: 10:1
Cardboard (shredded): 350:1	Garden waste (eg green prunings): 25:1
Newspaper (shredded): 175:1	Grass clippings: 20:1
Sawdust: 300:1	Hay: 20:1
Straw: 75:1	Horse and cow manure: 15:1
Wood ash: 25:1	Vegetable scraps: 20:1
Wood chips: 400:1	

BUILDING A YARD WASTE COMPOST BIN

By the time this bin is full, its contents will take three months to fully decompose. Use it for yard waste, like grass clippings and prunings. Don't add food scraps — put them in a sealed compost bin.

1 Drive two stakes in to hold up the first side. Do the same again with the second side.

2 Add the third side.

3 Add the fourth side. Put a safety cup on the top of each stake, then tie up the corners with tie wire or rope.

4 Fork uncomposted material onto the pile.

5 Add lawn clippings.

6 Mix urea into a bucket of water, then pour it over the pile.

decomposition. For a domestic compost pile, recycled wood pallets are ideal for a heap that's 1 cubic metre (1 cubic yard), a size that will process your garden and kitchen waste without taking up too much room. However, if you live in an area that's exposed to the elements — by the sea or in a windy area — make it a bit bigger, because the conditions will break it down faster. Nick down to your local bulk composting depot where pallets are chipped for making compost, and see if you can buy four of them.

I like to add some urea dissolved in water to my compost. This cheap, concentrated form of nitrogen (46 per cent) and ucleic acid allows micro-organisms to procreate. Use 1–1.5 kg (2.2–3.3 lb) urea to 1 cubic metre (1 cubic yard) of wood chips, which need nitrogen to rot. Make sure the pile is moist before pouring on the dissolved urea. In a few days, the temperature will rise.

Aerating your compost pile

Turn your pile regularly so that fresh air containing oxygen replaces oxygen-deficient air, otherwise the micro-organisms in the pile won't survive.

Store compost at different stages in a couple of plastic bins.

handy hint

You can speed up the decomposition process by reducing the raw materials into smaller pieces. For instance, shred a pile of leaves with the mower before you add them to the pile, or cut plant stems into smaller pieces with a pair of secateurs.

There are a few ways to do this. One is to simply turn the pile with a gardening fork or spade. Another is to add coarse materials such as leaves and stalks. You can buy aeration tools from garden centres or you can install a ventilator stack, made from bundles of sticks or tubes of chicken wire. Just make sure the stack sticks out the sides or top.

Adding moisture

Like all other living creatures, the organisms in your compost pile need water. Your pile should contain at least 40–60 per cent moisture. Below 40 per cent, the bacteria may become dormant; above 60 per cent, the pore spaces will become saturated and force out the aerobic bacteria, causing the pile to smell. You can ease this problem by adding dry carbon-rich material such as dead leaves and sticks. A general guide is to keep the composting material as damp as a squeezed sponge.

Judging when it's ready

Your finished compost should be about the same temperature as the ambient air temperature as well as crumbly and dark in colour, with a pleasant, earthy smell. There should be no lumps of undecomposed matter; if there are, it's not ready. If it's smelly and rotten, it may be toxic.

If you think it's ready, leave it for about three weeks to make sure it's stable. If you're impatient and work partly decomposed material into your soil, bacteria may compete with the roots for nitrogen and your plants will look

Use an aeration tool to turn your compost and get air pockets deep into the pile.

yellow and stunted. And if you're using it in a bed with seeds and seedlings, it could retard germination and the growth of your young plants.

Screening compost

It's a good idea to screen your compost before adding it to the garden. This process will isolate any large lumps that should be returned to the pile for a while longer so they can break down properly.

All you need to do is whack together a solid wooden frame and attach two layers of mesh — 5-cm (2-in) squares for the main mesh, overlaid with 1.5-cm (1/2-in) mesh, such as mouse, snake or aviary mesh. Of course you can get away with using a thicker gauged steel mesh, which then only requires one layer, but that stuff costs three times more than the two rolls of thinner gauged wire mesh I use. The thinner mesh is also more versatile than the rigid stuff: you can use it to protect seedlings and young plants from scratching chooks or wild rabbits.

Worm farms

Of course, not everyone has a garden big enough for a compost pile. If you live in a flat with even a small balcony, you have room for a worm farm, which is like a plastic carton in three layers. You can buy worm farms and tiger worms (*Eisenia fetida*) — worms from your garden prefer garden soil and won't thrive in a worm farm — from garden centres, or check if your local council stocks them.

Start by filling the top layer to about three-quarters full with a bedding of moistened shredded newspaper. Then bury food scraps (fruit and vegetables, coffee grounds, tea bags, crushed eggshells) and aged grass clippings in the bedding, which protects the food scraps from flies. Place the worms in the middle layer.

As the worms work their way through the top layer, keep adding more food scraps along with the occasional bit of water. The worm castings will collect in the bottom layer with the water, becoming a liquid compost that you can drain off and water on your plants.

Please note: worms don't like meat, banana, onion, garlic or citrus.

Did you know?

Earthworms are 72 per cent protein and less than 1 per cent fat. If they were prescribed as the only food in your diet, you'd probably lose weight.

MAKING A COMPOST SCREEN

The dimensions of this compost screen should be approximately 900 x 1200 mm (3 x 4 ft) so it fits neatly over a wheelbarrow.

1 Saw four pieces of 70 x 35 mm ($2\frac{3}{4}$ x $1\frac{1}{2}$ in) pine or use recycled timber — for example, from an old pallet. Two pieces should be 760 mm (30 in) and the other two 1200 mm (4 ft). Add galvanised angle brackets at each corner. Secure with self-drilling galvanised wood screws. Trim and neaten up the ends if necessary.

2 Using gang plates, attach 5-cm (2-in) wire to each corner and to the middle of each side of the frame.

3 Lay the finer mesh over the larger one. Fold over the rough edges of the finer mesh. Screw on lengths of pine to hold the 1.5-cm ($\frac{1}{2}$-in) mesh in place. You can unscrew and change the mesh later if you like.

4 Screen the compost. Use the fine stuff and return the bulk to the pile (or use it on the garden as mulch).

Common compost problems

It might take you a while to get the hang of making compost. The table below lists some common problems and how to solve them.

Compost tea

Compost tea is a liquid version of compost. What you do is add compost to a bucket of water, but the trick is that you have to keep the organisms alive while you make the tea. You can't just stand some compost in a bin of water for a week and then siphon off the liquid — you have to aerate it, just as you would a tank of tropical fish, so they have a constant supply of oxygen.

There are various bits of commercial equipment available for the job but I've worked out my own

Recycle kitchen waste by adding it to your compost pile.

SOLVING COMMON COMPOST PROBLEMS

Problem	Suggested solution
Big lumps that won't decompose	Avoid including corn cobs, eggshells, avocado seeds and pineapple tops unless you crush or shred them first
The pile smells	Too much nitrogen and not enough carbon. Add more carbon — dry, fibrous materials such as woody items and paper — and keep turning the pile regularly
Lots of ants and slaters	The pile is too dry, although the insects themselves aren't a problem. Sprinkle on some water or add less dry matter
Small flies, known as vinegar, compost or fruit flies (*Drosophila*)	Avoid leaving food scraps on the top — cover them with newspaper, dry material or a hessian bag
Vermin, blowflies or maggots	Don't add meat or fish Attach chicken wire to the bottom of the bin so rodents can't burrow underneath Bury food scraps under a layer of newspaper and/or grass clippings deep in the pile, about 20–30 cm (8–12 in) Top off the pile with a layer of dry leaves or grass clippings Keep the pile in the range of 54–71°C (130–160°F), where the thermophilic bacteria are active

step by step

MAKING COMPOST TEA

For this little project you'll need: 6 L (1½ gall) water in a bucket, 5-watt aquarium pump, 1 kg (2 lb 3 oz) well rotted compost, 1 tablespoon molasses and 1 tablespoon chicken manure.

1 Add compost to a bucket of water.

2 Add molasses and the chicken manure.

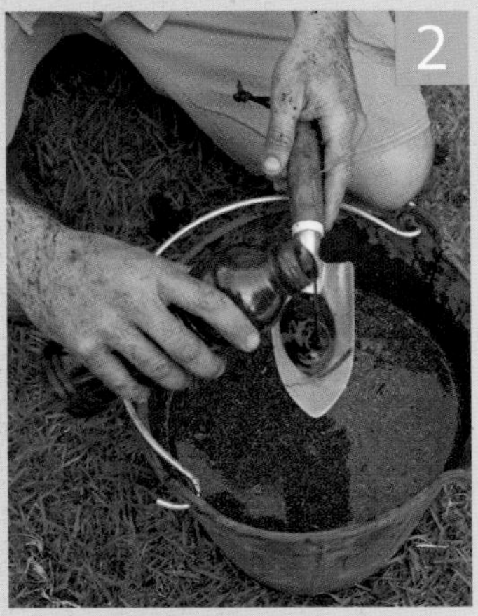

3 Place the pump in the water and leave it in a shady spot for 24 hours.

4 Sieve it before pouring it into a watering can and applying it to root zones or foliage.

method, using an aquarium pump. To every 20 L (5 gall) of water I add 1 kg (2 lb 4 oz) molasses. This feeds the organisms in the compost with sugar and carbohydrates and, if all goes well, their cells will divide every 15–20 minutes.

While we're talking molasses, it's wonderful stuff for nourishing the beneficial soil-borne organisms. Many beneficial fungi find it quite a turn-on: it increases their growth and reproduction rates considerably. These beneficial fungi greatly increase the health of the soil and plants as well as their resistance to pests and disease. One particular fungus, known as trichoderma, is quite effective in parasitising the eggs and juveniles of a terrible soil-dwelling pest known as root knot nematode or eelworm. An alternative method for controlling nematodes is to regularly incorporate extremely toxic chemicals into the soil. But be warned: nematicides are considered the most hazardous of all organophosphate chemicals and are easily inhaled, digested or absorbed through the skin.

So into a bucket put water, well rotted compost, molasses and a small handful of chicken manure, then agitate it with some kind of pump for about 24 hours. The chicken manure will provide extra nutrients while also raising the pH level of the tea. You can then apply it to soil, where it'll move into the root zone and supply nutrients to both the plant and the micro-organisms in the soil, or to foliage, where it will provide the leaves of the plant with beneficial micro-organisms and nutrients.

Compost tea acts more quickly than compost, but you must use only the best quality compost: any problems in the original compost, such as a high salt content, will remain, and even be compounded in the tea. You can store it for a week as long as you keep it in a shaded place with the tank constantly agitated and ventilated.

OPPOSITE Unlike the leaves of most trees, fallen oak leaves are rich in nitrogen and carbon, the essential ingredients for composting.

If you're adding stable waste to your compost, make sure it's well rotted before you use it to mulch your garden.

Remove any weeds before laying mulch.

Mulch

As I keep saying, mother nature provides us with a great guide to good gardening practices. Whenever you're out walking in the bush or a forest, you'll see the ground covered with fallen leaves and other types of plant litter. The natural environment copes pretty well with all this debris. It's not raked up and put out for council collection on the side of the road. Instead, it's left to rot down. This is mulch.

Benefits of mulch

Organic mulches soften the soil and improve aeration as they slowly decompose. Earthworms love the softer kind of mulches. It encourages them to do their thing in the topsoil, thus helping to create well structured and well drained soil. By maintaining the soil with these conditions you're providing the plant with extended periods of time to grow roots outwards and, most importantly, downwards.

If you mulch with a high quality compost, it will help control erosion and increase the soil's water retention, surface porosity and fertility.

You can use inorganic mulches too (see page 73), and both kinds are beneficial in the garden. Mulches:

- smother weeds;
- prevent weed seeds from germinating in bare soil and weeds from sprouting from below (as long as the mulch is deep enough);
- conserve moisture; and
- make a garden bed look neat and tidy, hiding any debris and rocks.

Organic mulches like straw protect vegetables such as squash, cucumber, unstaked tomatoes or strawberries, which all lie on the ground when they're ripe. (Now you know why they're called 'straw'-berries.) The mulch keeps them clean and dry, protecting them from rot and mildew. Likewise, low-growing flowers in a mulched flower bed won't be splashed with mud when the rains finally arrive.

Types of mulch

Many organic and inorganic materials can be used for mulch but I always use an organic one because it'll eventually break down, adding nutrients to the soil. In large public landscapes, landscape fabric or black plastic is often used beneath organic mulching materials to provide better weed control and to increase the mulch's ability to reduce water loss. I don't like them and I don't use them. Fabrics and plastics greatly reduce gaseous exchange. If a product claims the fabric allows sufficient air to pass through the soil then it must have holes big enough to allow weeds to grow through as well.

In shady areas, rock mulches control weeds and hold moisture, but in sunny spots, rocks tend to absorb and release heat over a longer period of time, which can increase water loss from nearby plants.

Organic mulches

These natural mulches should be fairly fine textured and non-matting. Straw, pine bark shreddings, bark nuggets, wood chips and other wood products are excellent materials for various effects in the landscape.

Grass

Grass decomposes rapidly and adds nitrogen to the soil, but don't mulch with more than 25 mm (1 in) of grass or it may heat up the soil enough to damage plants.

Hay and straw

Hay is inexpensive, decomposes rapidly and is a good source of nitrogen. However, it can add lots of weed seeds to the soil, so use second- or third-growth hay that hasn't gone to seed. Hay is cut from paddocks throughout the growing season. Second or third growth equates to how many times it's been cut in one growing season — that is, third growth has been cut and baled twice in the one year. Stockfeed suppliers have plenty of it. If you're prepared to drive out to the edge of suburbia and into farming lands, you'll find most of the products you need in greater quantities at less cost.

Straw looks good in a vegetable patch, is less weedy than hay and resists matting, even when it's wet, but be prepared for a possible mass germination of wheat or oats.

Premium lucerne hay is probably the best in this category. It decays rapidly, and herbs, roses and perennials love it. Buy it in bales, which contain far fewer weeds, and mix leaves with it. The high nitrogen levels in the lucerne complement the high carbon ratio of the leaves. The worms and other soil critters adore the stuff and can consume a 10-cm (6-in) layer within a month. It's also effective for controlling rose black spot and other fungal diseases.

handy hints

- *Don't mulch the soil around seedlings until they're well established: the high moisture content in the soil may encourage a fungal infection called damping off.*
- *When mulching around plants, leave a few centimetres around the stems or trunks to allow plenty of air circulation, otherwise they may suffer collar rot, another fungal infection.*
- *Don't mulch your perennials if the soil is waterlogged or, again, you'll end up with crown rot.*

If you're using fresh grass clippings as mulch, spread them thinly and mix them with leaves, otherwise the heat will build up.

With leaf and tree waste you don't know what you're getting — it could be diseased material or full of weed seeds.

Horticultural bark.

The trick is to continually spread layers of lucerne throughout the growing season. As the leaves infected with fungus fall to the ground, they're covered by another layer of lucerne. The soil's organisms rapidly devour the lucerne along with the diseased leaves and fungal pathogens.

Leaves

A 10–15-cm (4–6-in) layer of leaves forms an effective weed barrier. It also insulates the soil in winter and conserves water in summer. To improve the look of them, run them through a shredder before mulching.

Some aromatic plants — such as pine trees and camphor laurels — excrete volatile oils and alkaloids, which act as growth inhibitors. This is nature's way of inhibiting the growth of competing species. So if you want to use shredded waste from these plants, leave them to age for a month or so — but saying that, I've yet to experience any effects that outweigh the benefits of covering the soil with mulch. If you're going to use them repeatedly, I think it's always best to stockpile them for a while and then drench the pile with urea.

Recycled leaf and tree mulch

You can usually get this stuff for free from the tree contractors. A word of warning though! Many of these guys have minimal tree knowledge and, worse still, next to no understanding of how disease is spread.

Cypress bark canker is a perfect example of the risks associated with spreading a recently chipped diseased tree: an enormous quantity of fungal spores are blown into the surrounding atmosphere as the trees go through the shredder, and quite often the contractors leave the shreddings in situ. But worse still, the load of chips you're going to spread on your garden may be full of fungal spores. No wonder the disease is spreading like the plague.

Sugar cane

Bagasse, the fibrous residue of sugar cane, is a rapidly decomposing mulch used in tropical climates. As sugar cane lowers soil pH, lime is usually added at the same time. I also recommend using a dust mask when working with any of the softer mulches, as the fine dust particles and fibres can be very irritating.

Tree bark

This mulch can be either very chunky or finely ground or shredded for flower beds. It improves the soil as it decays but it can also remove nitrogen from the soil. If you use tree bark, I'd advise you to fertilise the soil with a slow-release form of nitrogen.

Toxic mulch

How can you tell if your mulch is toxic? Simply grab a handful and smell it. Toxic or sour mulch will smell like ammonia, sulfur, vinegar or silage, while sweet mulch should smell like good garden soil — just a nice, fresh, earthy smell. You can verify your olfactory findings by testing the mulch with a pH kit. Sour mulch is very acidic, with a pH of 1.8 to 3.6, whereas sweet mulch has a pH of 6 to 7.

The larger, chunky nuggets of bark can be a real nuisance in heavy rains as they float around like little boats. I go for either composted or uncomposted horticultural grade bark, which is used in potting mix and other soil media. Composted horticultural bark is my favourite as it doesn't create nitrogen drawdown problems and looks divine.

Wood chips

Wood chips look good and provide weed control, soil insulation and water conservation. However, as mother nature never intended for trees to be chipped up into uniform sizes then spread on her surface, she didn't have to consider how long it takes for them to decompose, thus borrowing nitrogen from the soil in the meantime. Wood chips should not be used near timber structures as they can attract termites.

Inorganic mulches

To be honest, I'm not a fan of any of these products. The fabrics can be helpful if you're working in areas with major perennial weed problems, but you just have to remember that the weeds will poke their heads out wherever light penetrates to the soil. And, of course, that area is usually where your desired species has been planted.

TOP When laying landscape fabric, cut x-shaped holes for plants.

BELOW Cypress pine wood chip is termite resistant but not sustainable unfortunately.

ABOVE Fine scoria (top) and Cowra white pebbles (bottom).

OPPOSITE In a Japanese garden, raked pebbles represent a calm sea, lending the landscape a meditative effect.

Geotextiles and landscape fabrics

These 'fabrics' are specially designed for gardens so they allow the soil to 'breathe' and water to infiltrate. They smother weeds, making them efficient mulches for large low-maintenance areas. If you're going to use landscape fabrics and you're irrigating the area, make sure you use drip irrigation and put it down before you install the fabric. Lay the fabric on bare soil, then cut x-shaped holes for plants. You'll need to attach the fabric to the soil with steel pins or tent pegs.

Rocks, pebbles and gravel

Pebble mulch was all the rage in the 1970s. If you've encountered it in recent times, chances are it was nearly impossible to dig: over time, the pebbles become covered with organic matter and soil particles, resulting in a material that's as hard as concrete. Even if you've recently installed pebble mulch, it won't stay looking good for long: leaves and other debris are difficult to remove and spoil the original effect. I suggest pebbles are best left out of the garden.

Not only does it take longer to apply these materials, but they also cause problems when you want to transplant shrubs or remove the mulch. Light-coloured materials will reflect sunlight and cause the temperature around the plants to rise. Rock mulch absorbs heat during the day and releases the heat at night, thus increasing the amount of water lost to evaporation, so avoid using rock mulch around plants that might not grow well under these conditions.

The only advantage I can think of is that these mulches don't decompose. If you do decide to use pebbles or gravel — perhaps for a rock garden or a Japanese-style one — install a border of some kind to keep the material in place, otherwise you may end up with rocks in the lawn or on the driveway and path. (And if you have young children, don't expect the pebble to stay neatly in place for more than a few minutes; in fact, pebbles and gravels could be safety hazards for small children.)

Black plastic

Don't use this in your garden. It won't let water, nutrients or air into the soil beneath, and any plants growing in a bed mulched with plastic will have shallow root systems.

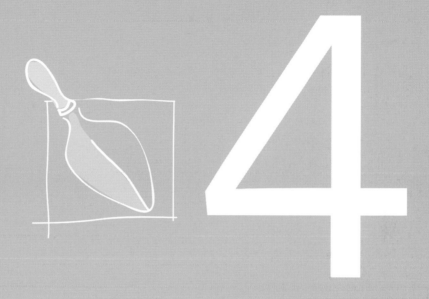

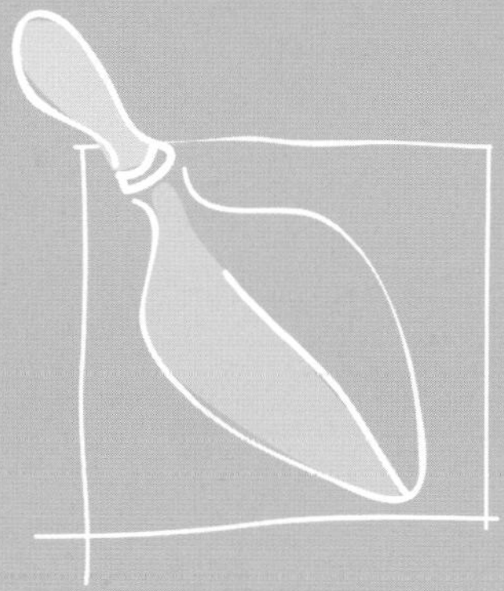

4

Water-efficient plants

Water-efficient plants

Well, you've finally made it to the point of what a garden is all about — plants.

By now the dirt you started with is soil, teeming with life, draining beautifully and smelling divine. You, on the other hand, are probably physically drained and looking a bit grubby, but feeling spiritually enriched by the whole experience.

So sleep well, safe in the thought that, provided you maintain a healthy layer of organic mulch to insulate the soil, worms and other wee critters will undertake the endless tasks of soil enrichment without any complaints.

Plants, soil and water

We've talked about the brown stuff. Now it's time to put it into context with the green stuff. If you don't remember the following information from your high school biology lessons, then it's time to refresh your memory.

Wetting front

Let's start the story during a lovely rainy day. When water is applied to the soil, it seeps down through the root zone very gradually. Each layer of soil must be filled to 'field capacity' before water descends to the next layer. That means that each layer must be saturated to the point where water runs off or puddles. This water movement is referred to as the 'wetting front'. Unless you've skipped a few chapters, you should know by now that water moves downwards through a sandy coarse soil much faster than it does through a fine-textured soil, such as clay or silt.

If only half the amount of water required for healthy growth in your garden or landscape is applied at a given time, it only penetrates the top half of the root zone; the area below the point where the wetting front stops remains dry as if no irrigation has been applied at all. This is where the trouble starts.

Once enough water is applied to move the wetting front into the root zone, moisture as well as dissolved nutrients are absorbed by the plant's roots and move up through the stem to the leaves and fruit. Just like your skin, leaves have thousands of microscopic pores, called stomata, located on the underside of leaves.

Water is constantly passing through the plant via the stomata in a process called transpiration. We've all seen a plant that's wilting and we all agree it doesn't look very happy. Believe it or not, wilting is the way most plants conserve water on very hot days or when soil water reserves are perilously low. Every stomata is surrounded by two guard cells. When things are getting dry down below or hot above ground, the guard cells are the first to lose water as it passes through the stomata. As the guard cells lose more and more water, they actually push the stomata into a closed position, thus greatly reducing the quantity of water lost during transpiration. Wilting also reduces the leaf's exposure to direct sunlight, which in turn further reduces water loss.

The temporarily stored water in the wilting leaves plays another vital role by providing a protective buffer for the plant's cells and tissues. If the above-ground temperatures continue to soar and the soil water availability isn't replenished, the guard cells gradually lose the water they're holding. Once it's all gone, there's nothing to protect the cells within the leaf. They dry out and the leaf stays floppy, often changing colour. At this

PREVIOUS SPREAD Blue-flowered pride of Madeira (*Echium fastuosum*) and the lime green lady's mantle (*Alchemilla mollis*) both perform well in temperate and Mediterranean climates.

OPPOSITE Tower of jewels (*Echium pininana*).

stage the poor thing has reached the point known as permanent wilt. Unless a constant supply of soil water is absorbed through the roots, this continual loss of water causes the plant to wilt.

Total water requirement

The total water requirement is the amount of water lost from the plant plus the amount evaporated from the soil. The combination of these two processes is called evapotranspiration. The amount of moisture loss depends on day length, temperature (both soil and air), cloud cover, wind, relative humidity, mulching and the type, size and number of plants growing in a given area.

Water is required for the normal physiological processes of all plants. It enables chemical reactions and the movement of substances through the various plant parts. Water is an essential component in photosynthesis and plant metabolism, including cell division and enlargement. It also cools the surfaces of land plants during the process of transpiration.

Nothing will inhibit a plant's performance faster than lack of water. It is the main factor determining harvest yields for all crops. Plants with insufficient water respond by closing the stomata, leaf rolling, changing leaf orientation and reducing leaf and stem growth as well as fruit yield.

Acacia sp. (left foreground), *Alternanthera* sp. (right foreground) and *Salvia microphylla* in the background.

Next time you endure a blistering heatwave with horrible drying winds, check out how your plants cope. You may notice that of two plants of identical species growing near each other, one may be scorched to a crisp while its neighbour made it through the day unscathed. In most cases, the latter had sufficient available moisture in the soil to absorb throughout the day while the crisp one had no moisture reserves to use in its defence. Once again, the tip is to pre-empt this by being an active smart gardener and watering plants early in the morning of a very hot day, rather than a reactive, not so smart gardener who only waters when you see wilting plants.

By the way, when you're going away from home for a while, never rely on a non-gardener to water your plants properly.

Identifying water-efficient plants

Before you spend a fortune on recreating a garden you've admired in a magazine, take the time to find out which types of plants suit your climate. There are many great plants that can perform well in a water-efficient garden.

So when you're choosing new plants for your garden, please look for plants that:

- store water;
- reduce water loss; or
- absorb water from deep in the soil.

Plants generally fall into three categories, depending on their capacity to get and conserve moisture. This is all about how plants manage their water requirements, not about how much water they require. In essence, we're looking at their physiology. When we discuss hydrozones or water requirements (see pages 176–83), we're talking about appetite.

Water spenders

Plants in this category transpire freely, but in deep soils they develop extensive root systems that absorb water from a large volume of soil. They will survive as long as some of their roots are in moist soil. Some of the most popular landscape plants are water spenders — for example, black walnut (*Juglans nigra*), London plane tree (*Platanus* x *acerifolia*) and mulberry (*Morus* sp.).

The leaves on this viburnum have changed colour because of environmental distress — in this case, not enough water.

Drought evaders

These plants have evolved a number of ways of avoiding water stress: they may become completely dormant in dry weather; they shed twigs and branches; or they simply drop leaves. However, while they have leaves, they transpire as freely as water spenders. Some examples of drought evaders are oyster plant (*Acanthus* sp.), Arum lilies (*Arum* sp.), naked ladies (*Amaryllis* sp.) and *Hosta* sp.

Water conservers

Typical of desert and Mediterranean climates, these plants have evolved various features that reduce water loss. For example, they may have small or leathery leaves, or grey or silver foliage, such as lamb's ears (*Stachys byzantina*). Its fine white hairs reflect the sun's rays and reduce the amount of water loss. Or they may have stomata that are structured to conserve moisture.

Some plants that are native to areas with hot, dry climates — such as Australia, South Africa, the Mediterranean and the west coast of America — have adapted to survive inhospitable conditions. Look for these features.

Leaf types

The colour, shape and surface of a plant's leaves are good guides to its ability to withstand moisture loss. Check out

LEFT *Amaryllis belladonna* dies back in summer to retain moisture.

OPPOSITE

TOP LEFT Once established, Australian natives can tolerate dry conditions and their roots grow deep. This group comprises lillypillies (*Syzygium* sp.), Gymea lily (*Doryanthes excelsa*) and *Westringia* sp.

BOTTOM LEFT *Vitex trifolia purpurea*, olive (*Olea* sp.), Italian and French lavender and white thyme (*Thymus serpyllum albus*) all do well in a Mediterranean climate.

TOP RIGHT New Zealand Christmas bush or pohutukawa (*Metrosideros excelsus*), cordyline, hebes and New Zealand flax (*Phormium tenax* 'Baby Bronze') are all natives of New Zealand. They require regular watering during the establishment period and well drained soil.

BOTTOM RIGHT Some irrigation is required for this collection of plants, all native to China — bamboo (various types), port wine magnolia (*Michelia figo*), *Gardenia* sp., Chinese star jasmine (*Trachelospermum jasminoides*), *Trachelospermum jasminoides* 'Tricolour', *Liriope* 'Evergreen Giant' and *Liriope* 'Silver Dragon'.

Did you know?

*Eucalypts (*Eucalyptus *sp.) position their leaves east–west rather than the usual north–south. In the northern hemisphere, the stomata face west to avoid the eastern sun; in the southern hemisphere, it's the reverse. This greatly reduces the surface area of each leaf that is directly exposed to heat and light, thus reducing the amount of water lost through transpiration.*

lavender (*Lavendula* sp.), with its small grey leaves; ivy-leafed geranium (*Pelargonium peltatum*), which has tough and waxy leaves; and zonal geranium (*Pelargonium* sp., Zonal Hybrids), which has thick and furry leaves.

LIGHT-COLOURED LEAVES High-water-use plants that thrive in shady areas have soft, dark green leaves, whereas water-efficient plants have light green, grey-green or blue-green foliage that reflects sunlight, reducing the amount of transpiration. Examples include lavender and cotton lavender (*Santolina* sp.).

SMALL LEAVES Most water-efficient plants, such as rosemary (*Rosmarinus* sp.), have small or needle-like leaves so that the minimum surface area is exposed to heat and light.

HAIRY LEAVES As I mentioned earlier, the hairs on leaves reflect the sun. They also reduce moisture loss by cutting down on the amount of air movement over the pores.

LEAVES WITH A TOUGH SURFACE Water-efficient plants may have a tough, waxy or leathery surface, which also cuts down on the amount of moisture loss. Many Australian native plants have tough leaves. Some examples are *Araucaria* sp. (which include the Norfolk Island pine), Wollemi pine (*Wollemia nobilis*), *Banksia* sp. and wax flowers (*Eriostemon* sp.)

PROTECTED STOMATA Water-efficient plants have fewer stomata, and most are on the underside of leaves, so they're protected from the sun and wind. Some examples are *Eucalyptus* sp., wattles (*Acacia* sp.) and *Grevillea* sp.

Strong internal structure

Water-efficient plants have a strong internal structure that prevents wilting in the heat. When combined with reduced transpiration, this feature means that these plants can survive long periods of heat stress. Tender plants wilt when they cannot take up water fast enough to replace moisture lost during transpiration. During prolonged hot and dry periods, excessive wilting can cause long-term structural damage.

Dusty miller (*Senecio cineraria*).

Persian shield (*Strobilanthes gossypinus*).

Kalanchoe sp.

Internal water sources

Water may be stored in many different parts of a plant, including the trunk (for example, the baobab tree, *Andansonia* sp., and barrel cactus, *Ferocactus* sp.); a swollen root system (kurrajong, *Brachychiton populneus*); or the leaves — pigface (*Portaluca grandiflora*), crassula (*Crassula* sp.) and kalanchoe (*Kalanchoe* sp.) all store water in this way.

Deep root systems

A deep root system enables a plant to reach deep into the ground in search of water. Some plants develop root systems that can tap into the water table, and once they're established, you don't need to water them. Some examples are ornamental and edible figs (*Ficus* sp.), Japanese windflower (*Anemone hupehensis*), junipers (*Juniperus* sp.), evening primrose (*Oenothera* sp.), comfrey (*Symphytum* sp.) and myrtles (*Myrtus* sp.).

Choosing a good plant

I have some ideas and you have the money, so let's visit some nurseries. There are lots of traps for young players though, so read this section carefully before you hand over the cash.

Shopping checklist

There are quite a few things to consider when you're shopping for plants. Damaged, diseased plants belong in the bargain bin. If you have a green thumb and a tight budget, by all means go ahead and try to nurse them back to health, but otherwise remember this wise proverb: 'buyer beware'.

QUALITY OF THE NURSERY If the majority of plants don't look healthy, find another nursery.

SHAPE Look for plants that are compact but full, with lots of stems. A plant that has had to strain for light in the nursery will be tall but spindly.

FOLIAGE Wilting or yellow leaves are a sign of stress, and you may not be able to nurse a stressed plant back to health once you get it home. Look for plants with healthy leaves.

BUDS AND FLOWERS While it may be tempting to buy plants that are already in flower, go for the ones that are still in bud. Remember this: when a plant's in flower, it's having sex! Imagine the extra strain on resources if you're settling into your new home and trying to make babies at the same time. It's all too much to bear. If your plants are not trying to procreate during this period, they'll recover from the transplantation process much faster.

STEM Old damage can weaken a plant. Take a look at the stem to make sure there are no cracks or scars.

INSECTS AND DISEASE Check the potting soil as well as both sides of the leaves to make sure the plant has no pests or diseases. Look for distorted leaves, black or sticky patches, mildew, holes and spots or scale.

ROOT SYSTEM If roots are growing out of the bottom of the pot, the plant is likely to be pot bound and may take a while to recover. Or, worse still, the tap roots may have grown around the circumference of the pot. The legacy of this becomes apparent years down the track. As these girdling roots thicken over time, they strangle the base of the plant. When this happens to trees, they blow over in windy conditions. When it happens to shrubs, they usually show signs of wilting stress, then cark it. On the other hand, if you can lift the plant out of the pot really

TOP This murraya is yellowing off, indicating a trace element deficiency, but the roots are fine.

MIDDLE Two lillypillies (*Acmena* sp.) showing fertiliser burn (left) and leaf scorch (right).

BOTTOM The cheese tree (*Glochidion ferdinandi*) on the left will be a good grower because it has roots with a collar above soil level. But the one on the right is planted too deeply. Unless you remove about 7 cm (3 in) of potting mix when you plant it out, it will probably develop a fungal rot disease such as collar rot (a fungus that grows in a damp environment and attacks the bark at the base of the plant). Although you can't see them here, the leaves are wilting. But hang on, there's plenty of moisture around the roots. What's happening is the fungus has attacked and blocked the vessels that carry resources from the roots to the leaves.

easily, it may not have been in the pot for long. In that case, leave it in the pot for a while before planting it out in the garden. If you're buying a tree or shrub wrapped in burlap, check that the root ball is solid. If there are any broken areas, it's likely that the roots have dried out.

WEEDS Weeds compete against the plant for nutrients and foster pests and disease.

The right mix

Another thing to look out for is good potting mix. First, run your fingers over the surface of the root ball or feel a small sample of the potting mix between your thumb and forefinger. You can quickly tell whether the potting mix is a soil- or sand-based medium as opposed to a compost-based type. Sand- or soil-based potting media are more compatible with garden soils, hold more water and are less likely to become hydrophobic when left to dry out. (Be careful when you're lifting soil- or sand-based pots, as they can be surprisingly heavy.)

If you're buying a plant for growing in garden soil, it's best to avoid compost-based potting mix. Why? First, and most importantly, if you're buying plants in autumn, it's quite likely they've dried out to wilting point during the summer heat. This problem is quite common with plants in pot sizes 15 cm (6 in) or smaller. It is especially

TOP LEFT Although the stem of this blueberry ash (*Elaeocarpus* sp.) is bent at the bottom, it'll straighten up as its girth thickens. Once again, it was buried too deep.

MIDDLE This prunus has been field grown and grafted onto inappropriate root stock. The feeder roots are a long way down.

TOP RIGHT The callused tissue on this brushbox (*Lophostemon* sp.) is showing signs of stake damage.

BELOW The root system on the plant at left is much healthier than that on the right.

TOP LEFT Here's a good example of what not to buy. The plant on the left is healthy but the one on the right has ant holes as well as wet and dry patches. It's also root bound (so much so, I had to cut the pot away).

TOP RIGHT This lillypilly was potted too deep by the grower and already has a case of collar rot.

ABOVE Notice how the roots don't grow in the ant holes.

OPPOSITE Many succculents protect their water reserves from grazing animals with sharp spines, which are modified leaves.

common in supermarket-style garden centres, where plant prices can be low due to minimal sales staff. The potting mix can be so soft and peat-like that when you plant your chosen specimen, the roots have to adapt to the radically different garden soil. This means the plant will take longer to establish itself. Be particularly conscious of the plant's water needs in the first three weeks after planting. You may need to water twice daily.

Container-grown planting techniques

Correct planting practices are yet another make or break factor. An old teacher of mine always repeated this pearl to me during planting projects: 'Lad, never spend a pound for the plant then only a penny for the hole you're sticking it in.' It took me a while to understand what the grumpy old mate was rabbiting on about, but I got the message eventually: the bigger the hole, and the more thoroughly it's prepared, the faster and better the plant's roots will develop.

Planting in the garden involves much more than just digging holes and dropping the plants in them. If you've practised smart gardening, then the soil will be already prepared, teeming with health and keen to welcome its new inhabitants. If you haven't practised smart

gardening, then remember that the existing soil is quite often compacted with poor drainage. It's essential to dig to improve both aeration and drainage. In clay- and silt-based soils, deep cultivation or digging is necessary to eliminate the hard pan that was probably formed below the soil surface during construction. To save you the hassle of flicking back some pages to soil preparation, here's a quick summary.

If you're planting trees and shrubs in large beds, prepare the whole bed rather than dig individual holes. That way, the roots will have a larger area in which to grow before they encounter native soil, which might be compacted and poorly aerated. To boost the amount of organic matter in the soil by 25 per cent, incorporate 75 mm (3 in) of composted or aged organic material, such as pine bark mulch or compost, into the top 30 cm (12 in) of soil. Never add uncomposted matter, or you may create nutrient deficiency problems or, worse still, toxic soil conditions.

handy hint

If you merely add organic matter to individual holes instead of preparing the entire bed properly, the plant's roots will become lazy and only inhabit the hole you've dug. During heavy rains, you'll also find that water will accumulate in the hole and drown the plant.

Estimating the quantity

Estimating the quantity of compost you'll need is pretty simple: basically, if your planting area is 100 square metres (120 square yards), and as I mentioned above, if you need to increase the quantity of organic matter by 25 per cent, then you'll need 75 mm (3 in) spread over the soil. Therefore you'll need to import 7.5 cubic metres (10 cubic yards) of compost. Fortunately for gardeners nowadays, most tips and landscape supply yards host bulk composting facilities and bulk compost sales.

Now, don't run out and order that amount of compost just yet. Make sure that the compost you're going to use has rotted thoroughly. The easiest way to determine this is to check its temperature. If it's warm, then it's still active. Use this stuff at your peril: at this stage of its life, it's actually toxic to plants and soil organisms.

Remember to take a soil sample and test it in a jar of water. In about an hour or so you'll have a pretty good idea of your existing soil's organic matter. My example of 25 per cent organic matter content was intended to make it easier to calculate. Aim for about 15 per cent organic matter. So to increase the organic matter by 15 per cent, you'll need 4.5 cubic metres (6 cubic yards) of compost.

LEFT These healthy white roots indicate this sweet pea is ready for planting out.

OPPOSITE Plant perennials like *Salvia* 'Majestic Spires' in groups so they don't look 'bitsy'.

Now remember to dig it thoroughly into the soil — really thoroughly! Clods of unmixed compost larger than a tennis ball are of no benefit to either the soil organisms or the plants.

So now your soil is well prepared and your plants are ready to go. Chances are the wee treasures have been growing in plastic bags or pots at the nursery. To follow is some advice on planting container-grown stock. Later on we'll discuss planting techniques for bare-rooted and root-balled stock.

Planting container-grown plants

These days, most plants are grown for sale in pots. Theoretically, they can be planted out year round, but if you plant container-grown stock in late autumn or early spring, the roots will have time to grow into the surrounding soil before summer, when high temperatures can damage new foliage.

My favourite time for planting is mid-autumn. The soil is still lovely and warm, and the stresses of summer are distant memories. The plant roots are busily growing

in all possible directions, seeking out moisture and nutrients. Meanwhile, above the soil, very little is happening. You may see a small amount of growth, but it'll be very little compared to what you see in spring.

The principal task of the leaves at this time of year is to photosynthesise the water and nutrients into sugars and starches. These will fuel the roots so they can grow as much as possible before the onset of colder weather.

The reduction in daylight hours is the messenger that informs the plants to prepare for the dormant period of the year. So, by the time winter comes around, you'll have all these plants, which were planted only a few months before, with root systems that are much larger in proportion to the green stuff on top. Come spring, the root system will be balanced by a strong flush of healthy, robust growth.

Another reason why I love to plant in autumn is that the establishment regimen is so much easier to manage. Plants require much less water than in spring. Providing your soil preparation was appropriate, the species you planted in autumn will have root balls nearly double in size and you won't have feeder roots inhabiting potting mix with garden soil surrounding it. Remember we discussed this earlier? Potting mix not only loses water due to the plant's consumption, it also loses water by capillary action. This in fact doubles the moisture loss of a container-grown root ball.

Sorry, I started to digress. Back to the topic of container-grown plants.

Digging the hole

Most new roots grow out horizontally from the root ball and, if watering has been insufficient, the bottom portion of the root ball dies. Concentrate on improving the soil towards the top 30–40 cm (12–16 in) from the surface and loosen or aerate the soil beneath to encourage those roots to grow as deeply as possible.

PREVIOUS SPREAD Pincushion flower (*Scabiosa columbaria*), *Dianthus* 'Doris' and *Rosa floribunda*.

RIGHT Tussock grass (*Poa labillardieri*) and in the background, *Lomandra longifolia*.

handy hint

When you're planting trees and shrubs, it's a good idea to build up a ring of soil around the outside edge of the hole. This stops any water from running off and keeps it in the root zone.

So, as I've said before, either prepare the entire bed (see pages 44–8) or dig really wide individual holes. As a general rule of thumb, dig a hole that is three times the width of the root ball, with sloping sides. Rough up the sides of the hole with a spade to make it irregular: if the soil is heavy and a little wet, the sides of the hole can become slick, inhibiting root growth and the movement of moisture.

Wherever possible, spread about 2.5 cm (1 in) of compost on top of the surrounding soil that you didn't prepare or dig, then give it a good going over with your garden fork. Push the fork in as deep as possible, then push it back and forth to create fractures and fissures within the soil horizon. After that, spread a generous layer of mulch over it. You can go thicker than 8 cm (3 in) in these outer areas. By doing this, you're providing the resources needed by mother nature to improve the soil environment in her own time.

Fill the hole with water and let it drain completely before you plant. This practice both reduces the effects of capillary action from the backfill soil and also determines whether the soil drains well enough to accommodate the species you're planting.

Planting technique

Now the hole's dug, let's look at what you need to do with the plants.

1 Soak the plants in a tub of water mixed with a good dollop of molasses. A children's wading pool is ideal.
2 To remove the plant from the pot, turn it upside down and tap the bottom of the pot so that the root ball falls into your hands. If the plant is pot bound, cut away the pot so you don't place pressure on the stem base. Pulling on the trunk or stem can split or break the tap roots and damage the fine root hairs.
3 Loosen the roots before planting. If the roots are only slightly encircled, you can loosen and spread them out by hand. If the thicker roots are girdling the root ball, then more brutal actions are required. Carry out step 4 below, and once you're satisfied with the plant's position in the hole, take to the outer root ball with your secateurs, gently cutting your way into the centre of the root ball. What you're looking for are any tap roots thicker than a tube of lipstick that are circumnavigating the root ball. When you locate one, carefully cut through the root and gently bend it out, away from the plant. Some roots will flick back to resume their journey. Cut those back further. It's quite possible that you'll end up with a root ball that's been cut right open. I think chefs call it 'butterflying'. This activity will almost certainly reduce the amount of foliage growth the plant will achieve that year, but the sacrifice will be well worth the effort in years to come, especially if you're planting trees for the next few generations to appreciate.
4 Pick up the plant by its root ball and place it in the hole. Make sure the plant is straight and at the right depth (see 'Checking the planting depth' on page 99). If the top of the root ball is higher than the soil surface, water may not soak down into the root ball. If the root ball's too deep, it will suffocate the root system and/or encourage fungal disease.
5 If the soil looks like it needs it, incorporate some organic matter into the backfill (the soil you removed from the hole) and loosen any clumps, which can allow air pockets to form around the root ball. If a soil test shows that you need it, add lime to the backfill, but don't add fertiliser because, at worst, it could burn the roots and, at best, make them too lazy to travel into the soil.
6 Once the hole is one-third full, firm around the root ball with your hands. If you use your boots with some of your body weight behind them you could end up causing the soil to compact. Top up the hole.

PLANTING

Make sure you soak the plants before planting them. If they're dry when you put them in the soil, their root balls won't be able to absorb water.

1 Fill a large bin (or a child's sandpit shell, as shown) and add seaweed extract.

2 Add the plants in their pots. If they're dry, bubbles of air will escape and you may have to hold them down.

3 Dig compost and either a handful of dolomite or lime (not both) into as much of the garden soil as possible.

4 Dig the hole, water it and then pop in the plant. Make sure you get the level right.

5 Backfill, and firm it with your hands. Check the level again.

6 Water in with diluted molasses or compost tea (see page 68) — 3–5 L (5–9 pints) per plant if it's really sandy soil — and finish with a thick layer of mulch. Dilute the molasses or compost tea at a rate of 5–20 mL per litre ($1\frac{1}{2}$ teaspoons–$1\frac{1}{2}$ tablespoons per 2 pints) of water.

7 Water the plant. This will eliminate air pockets around the roots. Mound a ring of soil above the edge of the root ball to reduce runoff during future watering sessions. Add an 8-cm (3-in) layer of mulch around the plant but take care to keep it away from the plant's stem or trunk. As the plant grows, keep replenishing the mulch and extending the area it covers.

Planting in poorly drained sites

If you're planting into a poorly drained site, there are a couple of things you can do to help the plant establish itself. One option is to dig the hole to about two-thirds the depth of the root ball and place the plant in the hole so that it's slightly above the soil level. Mound the soil around the root ball so that it's five times wider and falls away in a gentle slope.

The other method is to simply loosen the soil for an extra 3–5 m (10–15 ft) beyond the hole. This will greatly improve the plant's chances of sending roots into the surrounding soil.

What about pruning?

You can prune any parts damaged by the planting process, but otherwise leave the plant alone! It used to be the norm to prune after planting, but times have changed. Every leaf that's left on the new plant increases its ability to photosynthesise water and nutrients into sugars and starches. The more sugars and starches are made available to the roots, the more the roots can perform cell division and grow further and further into the ground you prepared earlier. It makes simple sense when you think about it.

Planting balled and burlap trees

First off, burlap is a big sheet of hessian that's wrapped around the root ball to stop the soil falling away from the root system and, of course, from drying out.

A popular and efficient nursery practice is to field grow trees and shrubs. Some growers stick the young plants in synthetic root control bags, then plant them out in the field for a year or two. The old school approach is to plant them without the bags and root prune the plants instead. Either way the intention is

Checking the planting depth

Make sure the planting depth is exactly the same depth as it was in the container by determining the root ball depth before you plant.

1 Rub off any excess loose potting mix from the top of the root ball until you expose the thicker roots at the base of the plant.

2 Hold a stick beside the root ball and place your hand on the stick where it's level with the root ball.

3 Place the stick in the planting hole, which should not be any deeper than the root ball. The loosened soil below the root ball can settle, resulting in the plant being planted too deep. Or place a stick across the hole, as shown below.

4 If the hole is too deep, firm the bottom of the hole to reduce settling.

Checking the planting depth.

to ensure that the root ball is dense, well branched and situated directly beneath the foliage.

The nursery usually lifts these plants in late autumn and through winter, then either sells them as they are or pots them into bigger containers and sells them later as advanced stock. In the cooler temperate climates, this is the standard method for growing and selling evergreen trees and shrubs. You can pick up some excellent bargains buying balled and burlapped plants. Converting the bargains into healthy garden plants requires a little more effort than planting container-grown plants, but if you follow my advice you should be right.

Before I start, there are some golden rules. Break these and you'll probably blow your money.

1 Never, ever, let the root ball dry out.
2 Never, ever, lift or carry the plant from the trunk or stem, as the weight of the soil will tear or snap the roots. Always lift and carry the root ball.

Now you know how to treat the plant, here's what you do with it.

1 Dig and prepare the ground as you would for container-grown plants.
2 Gently lower the plant into the ground.
3 Remove the material surrounding the root ball with sharp scissors or a utility knife. Be careful though — it's tough material.
4 Have a good look at the root system for things like broken or split roots and root girdling. If these are present, carefully prune the damaged or offending girdling roots.
5 Place the backfill soil carefully around the root ball and firm in with your hands, not your boots.
6 Keep the root ball moist, but not soaked, for the establishment period.

Planting bare-rooted plants

If you live in a region that's blessed with a dormant winter and you're on the prowl for deciduous trees, shrubs, roses and climbers, this is the method for you. Although bare-rooted plants are seldom seen in retail garden centres, they remain popular with mail order nurseries, in particular rose and fruit tree suppliers. The plants are grown in the field for one to four years, root pruned during the growing season, if necessary, and lifted in early winter for grading and despatch.

Lower the plant into the hole before unwrapping and removing the burlap or hessian.

Planting bare-rooted plants is a tad different from planting container-grown plants, as there's no soil around the roots. It's very important that you plant them as soon as possible and never let their roots dry out. About 30 minutes before planting time, pop the plants in a bucket of water with a good dollop of molasses mixed through (the sugars will assist root growth).

1 Once again, prepare the soil to the best of your ability, then dig a hole about 30 cm (12 in) deep.
2 Backfill so the roots are sitting on the firmed soil beneath and the base of the stem is level with the surrounding ground.
3 Make a little mound or volcano shape in the bottom of the hole for the thicker roots to straddle (this reduces the risk of having large cavities of air around the roots).
4 Inspect the plant for any damaged or broken roots. Prune these bits off, but try to retain as much undamaged root structure as possible.
5 Place the plant in the hole with its thicker roots straddling the mound of soil, so they are pointing away from the plant in as many directions as possible.

6 Pop a stake in the ground to support the plant, then gently backfill and firm the soil with your hands. Keep it moist, but not soaked, until the following autumn.

If you're caught short and don't have time to plant a bare-rooted plant immediately, find a pot that accommodates its roots and pot it up with a decent potting mix. As long as you look after it, it will happily grow on in spring and can be planted any time.

Obstacles to growth

It's important for the roots to be uninhibited by urban structures — such as concrete footings, pathways, planter boxes and roads — or natural obstacles, such as underground boulders, tree stumps and large roots. If it has to cope with many of these structures or obstacles, the plant may require ongoing love and attention.

Plant establishment

Before we start talking about this make or break topic, I need to emphasise the importance of water and, more importantly, how you deliver it to new plantings. Believe me, there's a huge difference between irrigating by hand and irrigating via a designed system.

Another thing I should mention is that in order to achieve a healthy, water-efficient garden, in the next 12 months you'll use a considerable quantity of water — in fact, thousands and thousands of litres or gallons of the precious clear liquid. If you fail to provide the recent plantings with their initial water needs, then I can guarantee that your garden's future water consumption will be hundreds of times greater, and you will be fighting disease and pestilence while at the same time advertising to friends and neighbours your lack of gardening skill.

An established tree or shrub has many roots that have grown a distance equal to approximately three times the radius of the canopy. Don't be concerned if the shoots and trunk are growing more slowly during the establishment period than they did before going into the ground. This is due to the love that nurseries lavish on their stock. Like farmers, nurseries ensure their crop never goes without. The stress of suddenly going from a protected, loving environment into a situation with far less protection is considerable.

If you've engaged the services of a landscape contractor or unqualified gardener instead of a practising horticulturalist to do your planting, then watch them like a hawk. If they fail to provide the plants with the necessary care for reducing the stress and shock of entering the new environment, then it's quite likely the plant will never develop into the specimen either you envisaged or they promised.

Every organism knows what to do to survive. Plants are no different: their roots are given priority. For the first year or so after planting, the above-ground growth will be negligible compared to the growth underground. Providing there are enough leaves to absorb sunlight and convert it into sugars and starches, the plant will be happy. The growth rates above ground will relate directly to the growth rates below ground. Failing to provide enough of the primary needs of water and air and also the secondary needs — nutrients to the roots — can result in the death of a large portion of the root ball.

Imagine this for a tick. When removed from its container, the plant's root ball is 25 cm (10 in) top to bottom. You then stick it in the ground and provide only enough water to wet the top half 12.5 cm (5 in) of the root ball and surrounding soil. Because of your actions — or, more to the point, your inactions — you have obliged the plant to adapt to its new watering regimen. It will shut down the lower half of its root ball because there are no resources for it to exploit. Meanwhile, the shoots and leaves up top are still demanding water and nutrients for photosynthesis but, sadly, there are now only 50–75 per cent fewer roots to absorb the required resources. Next thing you know, the leaves and shoots will get smaller, pests and diseases will take hold, growth

Container plants and soil root space

Planter boxes, tubs and other containers are all the rage now, especially in inner city developments. But many landscape architects and designers are living in fantasy land when they recommend planting large shrubs or small trees in shallow, concrete planter boxes. These plants are positioned to provide shade and privacy, reduce noise or wind and generally improve the value of the property. This is certainly the case when the soil volume is sufficient to accommodate a root ball that can sustain the vegetation above ground. Once again, it's an example of 'guesswork' rather than 'homework'. Never, ever, regard the specimen growing in a planter box as established. Please treat it as a pot plant and care for it accordingly.

This kind of potted display will require supplementary irrigation and replanting every five years or so.

Calculating root space

Deciding what plants to grow in tubs, large pots or planter boxes usually begins with listing plants that have the desired size and shape to accommodate the position, but does the position have enough space to accommodate the plant? If you only consider the above-ground space, then you're only considering your needs, not the plant's. We all know that relationships rarely prosper when a selfish party is involved. The plant needs enough root space in the soil to produce enough foliage to serve your needs. Root space is seldom considered in the garden and virtually never considered in container planting.

It's easy to assess whether you have adequate above-ground space — just research the species's mature shape and size, and then make sure you have enough room for it. Rooting space is a little trickier. Below is a mathematical equation that can give you a general idea of the soil you need. But remember this: if you have a compacted layer in your soil, then you can't consider any soil beyond that layer as usable root space. So I'll repeat my previous advice: before you visit the nurseries, dig a hole to determine the soil depth, structure and texture and, most importantly, eliminate any compacted layers of soil.

Crown projection

In the industry, the area of the circle of ground covered by a tree's canopy is known as 'crown projection'. You can calculate crown projection by taking the mature crown spread of the tree, squaring it and multiplying by 0.7854.

The magnificent royal poinciana (*Delonix regia*).

The planting area should have 0.05 cubic metres (2 cubic feet) of soil available for rooting for every 0.09 square metres (1 square foot) of crown projection. For example, a mature tree with a canopy spread of 10 m will have a crown projection of $10^2 \times 0.7854 =$ 78.54, and $78.54 \div 0.9 \times 0.5 = 43.633$ cubic metres of usable soil volume for root growth. In an average soil, you can expect roots to penetrate 1 m (3 ft). Use this standard depth as one of the three dimensions of a volume of soil. (In imperial measurements, if your canopy spread is 30 feet, that'll work out as a crown projection of $30^2 \times 0.7854 = 707$, and $707 \times 2 =$ 1414 cubic feet of soil volume.)

Back to our example: the square root of 78.54 cubic metres is 8.86 m. This means you'd need a soil volume with dimensions of 8.86 x 8.86 x 1 metre soil depth to ensure adequate soil space for the tree in this example. (In imperial measurements, you're looking at 29 x 29 x 3 feet soil depth.)

Planting a hedge into a trench will guarantee consistent growth and a long life.

will die back and you've blown your money. This scenario happens more often than not, especially in gardens that are planted in spring and summer.

Once a tree or shrub's growth rate has become more or less consistent from one year to the next, it's considered established. By the end of the establishment period, and providing you've matched the species needs with what your climate provides, it will have grown enough roots into the surrounding garden soil to keep it alive without supplementary water.

Watering during the establishment period

The idea here is to provide the plant with enough water during the first growing season after transplanting so that it can establish its roots into the surrounding soil and develop strong and healthy leaders or stems. So for trees and shrubs, allow three months for every 25 mm (1 in) of trunk diameter. Therefore, a tree that's 15 cm (6 in) in diameter will need 18 months to establish itself.

Be prepared to irrigate through the entire establishment period, especially during drought. Since most root growth occurs in the warmest months, be sure that the soil moisture is appropriate during this crucial season. This means you need to apply about 8 L (2 gall) of water for every 25 mm (1 in) of trunk diameter. When you're doing the right thing and catering for the

PLANTING A HEDGEROW

Prepare the planting bed in accordance with my previous instructions (see pages 44–8). *Viburnum odoratissimum*, an evergreen shrub with fragrant flowers in spring, was used for this hedge.

1 Soak the plants in a tub of water. The root ball of each plant should be drenched.

2 Dig a trench to ensure the plants will be in a straight line and at the same depth, and check there are no obstructions. Soak the ground where you're going to plant the hedge.

3 Position them — in this case 60 cm (2 ft) apart. This will be a lower hedge, so you need to minimise the gaps.

4 Remove all excess soil and tease out the roots.

5 Dig the hole and position the plant in the trench. Lay a spade or broomstick across the trench to check the soil level.

6 Backfill until the plants are halfway in, then if the soil is really dry, water again. This will also remove air pockets from the backfill.

7 Finish backfilling. Firm the soil around each plant with your hands. Water again.

8 Then mulch with what you have on hand.

Condensing your perennial plantings will reduce maintenance and provide a wonderful effect.

plant's needs, the root growth is quite amazing. I'm not exaggerating: the fine roots of many plants can grow 25–50 mm (1–2 in) a day. I find this mind-blowing, as this phenomenal growth is due to each cell growing, then dividing, over and over again.

Unfortunately, most trees are under-irrigated during the establishment period, and consequently they develop low, co-dominant stems and double leaders that may eventually split off. If you underwater your plants during the first warm season after transplanting, you could lose an entire season's root growth.

The watering regimen outlined on the next page is intended as a general guide. When you're determining the volume and frequency of each watering session, you must also consider the season and local conditions such as wind, shade, rainfall patterns, soil types, temperature range and aspect.

If you follow this establishment regimen but you've prepared the soil with a 'she'll be right' approach, then you may find that some plants will become waterlogged and possibly die. Should this happen, it's nobody's fault

You can always use the mower to achieve some interesting effects, such as a clipped seating area in a meadow.

RECOMMENDED WATERING REGIMEN FOR SPRING AND SUMMER	
Month (after transplanting)	Frequency
First	Daily
Second	Every other day
Third	Twice a week
Fourth	Once a week until plants fully established

HOW MUCH TO WATER	
Pot size	Quantity of water
150 mm (6 in)	1.5 L (3 pt)
200 mm (8 in)	2.5 L (3/4 gall)
250–300 mm (10–12 in)	5 L (1 1/2 gall)

but your own. The positive thing about this possible scenario is that at least the plants will have died when they're small. There's nothing more disappointing than seeing plants fail when the garden's entering its advanced or mature era.

Weeding

Now listen to this sermon. Remove all weeds as soon as they appear. Why? Remember that all plants compete for sunlight, water, nutrients and soil. While a weed is growing beside your plant or within your prepared and mulched areas, it's robbing the garden of resources that your plants would otherwise have access to.

Water-efficient lawns

Before we start, I need to make one thing clear. We are in the business of creating a lawn, not grass. A lawn.

I can hear you saying, 'Some television experts have told me that grass is a water guzzler and that I should rid myself of this environmental glutton.' Yes, in situations where it's managed poorly, grass consumes more water than most garden plants. Why?

When a plant has thousands of leaves exposed to the sun at any one time, and they're sheared off within an inch of their life every week or so, it ends up with a shallow root system. So it's no surprise it needs regular watering to keep it green and weed-free.

I'll let you in on another bit of info. Only in gardens tended by humans will you see grass surviving with such a shallow root system and at the same time coping with regular trimming and traffic. Think about the types of grasses that grow on prairies or in paddocks, exposed to a whole gamut of extreme weather. In these environments, herbivores often browse the grasses much shorter than a lawn and, as they chomp away, they couldn't give a hoot about the survival of the grass they're consuming. If they rip up the plant, roots and all, then it dies. Natural selection dictates that only the most suitable and adaptable species can survive the hazards of life on earth.

How do these close relatives of our turf grasses survive? Simply by evolving to have a root system that can grow deep and hold tight. And at certain times of the year, most natural grasses experience a dormant period due to climatic factors. On the African savannah, grasses are dormant in the dry season, while in temperate zones, winter can be the time for rest.

With that in mind, ask yourself whether you think it's okay for your lawn or grass to shut down or become dormant during periods of unfavourable weather. If you can see the soil surface within your grass, then a long period of summer drought dormancy is quite likely to kill it off. On the other hand, if your lawn has dense, healthy growth with roots growing to depths of 45 cm (18 in), then you'll find that the lawn can brown off for a while then kick back into action when favourable conditions again prevail.

You can encourage an extensive, deep root system by accurately supplying appropriate quantities of water (more on this a bit later). You can also increase the mowing height and keep the blades of your mower sharp so that the lawn has more leaf area with which to absorb sunlight and so suffers less stress. Grass behaves like bonsai: if you keep the growth short, the roots will naturally stay short too. And yes, you guessed it: if you ensure the soil and its fertility are finely tuned and well adjusted, the roots will grow deep.

Years ago, I worked with a cranky old greenkeeper. He had an unpleasant manner towards people but he was devoted to his lawn. He never greeted me or bade me farewell, but throughout the working day he would mumble turf grass philosophies to the point of spouting clichés. The one that's etched in my mind went something like this: 'The beauty is in the blades, but the action is in the roots.' The point I'm trying to make is that turf grass is just another kind of plant. If you provide it with the right conditions, it will grow well, be water efficient and cope better with the stresses of extended dry times.

handy hint

Water the root ball, not soil that's more than 50 cm (20 in) away from it. If you're not sure if it needs water, stick your finger in the soil. And finally, don't water a saturated root ball, especially in the first three months.

Getting serious about preparation

So we've established that, depending on the soil conditions and your cultural practices, your turf grass will develop extensive deep root systems. The health and quality of the lawn reflect the health and quality of what it's growing in. Before any planting takes place, you must prepare your site properly and improve the soil. If you're planning to lay turf yourself then you've probably obtained soil preparation instructions from the internet or a glossy turf sales brochure. The overwhelming majority of turf soil preparation instructions I've read make me want to shake my fists with fury.

Here's some preparation advice from the commercial sector of the industry, followed by my rebuttals.

- 'On most occasions, it's not necessary to improve the soil.' Excuse me? On all occasions, it's important to improve the soil.
- 'If the area is clayey you should apply some gypsum.' Don't bother unless you're working with a clay soil with a high sodium content. Even then you'll need to apply the stuff at least once a year.
- 'If your yard has a clay base you will need to add topsoil mixture.' And? If you dump a sandy soil mix over a clay base, the grass roots won't even grow to the depth of the topsoil.
- 'It may be easier to hire a bobcat to prepare the soil.' Not on your Nelly! Bobcats or skid-steer loaders compact the soil with gusto. (I'll discuss the alternative in a tick.)
- 'Rotary hoe the soil to a depth of 10–15 cm (4–6 in), then level the soil with a rake.' In the wrong hands, rotary hoes can create a whole new range of future hassles.

It's ironic that sales pitches always paint a picture of ease and simplicity. The preparation advice offered above

ABOVE This grass looks green and healthy enough, but some patches are starting to die off and it's not hard to see why – the soil hasn't been prepared properly. The topsoil layer is very thin and just sitting on top of the subsoil.

PREVIOUS SPREAD This garden may look as if it belongs in a temperate climate but it's actually in the subtropics.

by the commercial sector works reasonably well if you have the water to splash on it every few days or so. It may look green and lush but it'll have a root system that occupies only the top 10 cm (4 in) of the soil. During the next extended rainy period, it'll begin to fail from either waterlogging or compaction. It's basically all façade, with no real muscle behind it.

Let's face it — the urban landscape industry worldwide is loaded with businesses that care very little for the longevity and efficiencies of their finished product or have very little understanding of the science of growing plants. I regularly visit recently completed gardens to determine and remedy the plant and soil problems that should have been addressed long before the plants went in. The costs associated with redoing an area of a garden that should've been prepared properly the first time round can be astronomical. The solution is to eliminate the guesswork and leave nothing to chance.

Getting the soil right

Loams, sandy loams and loamy sands, with a pH of 6.0 to 7.0, are the very best soils for producing a beautiful, high-use, low-maintenance lawn. Unfortunately, this ideal soil mixture is rarely found on any property after construction. You're more likely to be faced with an area that would better suit a highway — that is, layers of compacted soils that bear little resemblance to what you and I know as soil. In fact, this is what you'd call dirt. If the plan is to re-turf in an existing garden, follow the same steps below and pretend that the existing grass is the debris. The method below guarantees success and, compared to the punters' methods I outlined before, will reduce the turf's water requirements by up to 40 per cent.

First, we must obey the golden rule: if the soil is wet, we're not going to work with it.

Steps 1 and 2 below are universal for all soil types. After that, we need to split up and discuss the methods for well drained subsoils on the one hand and not so well drained subsoils on the other.

1 Clear the site

Clear the site of everything that doesn't resemble soil — for example, builders' waste, rocks, gravel and anything else that's larger than a golf ball. If the job is big enough for a digger machine, then you can hire an operator who has both a skid-steer loader (with caterpillar tracks so it won't compact the soil) and a mini-excavator. For the small extra cost per hour, the job will be more accurate. The excavator will scrape the waste into a pile for the skid-steer to ferry away. This will ensure the skid-steer uses the same path, in and out, all day long. The excessive soil compaction created by the skid-steer will be ripped open by the excavator as it reverses off site.

If the topsoil resembles sandy loam, remove it and stockpile it for re-use.

2 Level the site

OK, let's assume the subsoil drainage is fine. Using either the excavator or a hard rake, roughly grade the entire subsoil area to a consistent level. This includes sloping the grade away from building foundations, eliminating or reducing severe slopes and filling any low-lying areas.

Test the drainage

Before the subsoil is disturbed, you must collect some soil samples to determine the pH, texture and structure (see 'All about soil', pages 19–25). Then dig a few holes 10 cm (4 in) deep and 40 cm (16 in) wide into the uncompacted subsoils. These holes should be in different areas of the proposed lawn — say, one at a low point, one at a higher point and one where you think the most foot traffic will occur.

Fill them with water to a depth of 2.5 cm (1 in) and measure the time they take to drain. If it takes more than an hour for 5 mm ($^1/_4$ in) to drain away, then you'll need to install subsurface drainage (see pages 20–1).

There will be more rubbish to remove once you've completed this task.

Depending on the size of the area and how many helpers you have, it should be getting near lunchtime. If none of the spectators indoors is offering you a cup of tea, knock on the door and ask them what letter comes after S in the alphabet. As soon as you hear them reply 'T', quickly snap back: 'That would be lovely, thank you.'

While we're having lunch, let me give you the drum on why this method grows better lawns. We now know that roots will happily grow into soils with enough moisture and enough air for them to seek out the dissolved nutrients in the water. Once the soil dries out, so do the nutrients. Our mission is to invite the lawn's roots to venture, without hindrance, as deep as their genetic make-up will allow, so they can exploit a greater volume of moisture-holding soil. Like trees and shrubs, when turf has roots to these depths, it can draw on moisture reserves to maintain survival during extended dry periods.

Now you can understand why the popular industry practice of spreading 10 cm (4 in) of friable soil over uncultivated subsoils is a disgraceful practice.

Surprisingly, some popular turf varieties can reach depths like the ones in the table below.

Now, keep in mind that roots will achieve these depths *if*:

- physical resistance is eliminated;
- the air-filled porosity is suitable, and
- the supply of water is sufficient.

3 Open up the soil

Regardless of the type of subsoil you have, you need to open it up sufficiently to allow the sandy loam turf soil to blend into the subsoil. But only do this work when the soil is dry: it's vital that the subsoil shatters and cracks into smaller aggregates. If the subsoil is clay based and it's wet, don't do it: ripping will smear or press the clay

WARM-SEASON GRASSES		COOL-SEASON GRASSES	
Type	Depth of roots	Type	Depth of roots
Common couch grass	48–60 cm (19–24 in)	Tall fescue	75 cm (30 in)
Hybrid couch grasses	60–98 cm (24–39 in)	Kentucky blue grass	45 cm (18 in)
Zoysia grasses	24–48 cm (9–19 in)	Bent grasses	20 cm (8 in)
Soft-leaved buffalo grasses	32–48 cm (13–19 in)		

Rosemary and lavender need savage pruning twice a year so they don't get leggy.

particles together, resulting in a claggy ball of trouble. As I've said before, unless the subsoil has a high sodium content, you're wasting your time and money spreading gypsum on clay soils.

I reckon it's best to use a machine for the ripping stage. For very heavy or post-construction site soils, the skid-steer is totally useless, but the excavator will do a brilliant job and the electric jackhammer with clay spade is also highly effective. If the subsoil is more like sandy clay loam, then a heavy-duty garden fork should do the job. Remember that the deeper and more thoroughly you rip, the better your lawn will be. See page 44.

4 Take care

Now the challenge is to ensure that once you've opened up the subsoil as deeply as possible — to a minimum depth of 20 cm (8 in) — you need to do a couple of things to keep it open: keep heavy machinery off it, and always walk on planks or boards. If you don't follow this advice and the soil's wet, you will destroy the structure and drainage.

The best turfing soil for domestic lawns

What you need is a free-draining medium to achieve a minimum total topsoil depth of 20 cm (8 in) after firming. The topsoil should be a loamy sand, sandy loam, clay loam, loam, silt loam, sandy clay loam or other soil suitable for the area. If you can, incorporate humus (fully decomposed organic matter) into the topsoil.

But first do a quick jar test of the soil to determine the quantity of sand, silt and clays in the soil (see page 17). If the clay content is less than 10 per cent, add 10 per cent zeolite to the total volume of soil. One tonne (1 ton) will be sufficient for 10 tonnes (10 tons) of sandy loam. The zeolite will behave much like clay and humus colloids, and it will greatly reduce nutrient runoff and increase the soil's water-holding capacity.

If the clay content is 5 per cent, then add 15 per cent zeolite once you've spread the topsoil to the required 20 cm (8 in) depth throughout the lawn area. Then rake it into the topsoil before you do the final screed. The trick is to carefully spread the topsoil over the deep ripped subsoil to allow the subsoil and topsoil to blend without an obvious layer forming between the two soils. This will help both the roots and the water to move into the subsoil.

If the subsoil settles again, gently open it up and allow the topsoil to fall into the subsoil voids. This is the key. You must allow as much topsoil as possible to gain access to the cracks and fissures within the subsoil.

Once you've got your topsoil levels right, you can water the area. This will make the soil settle, indicating where you need to top it up. Once your levels are correct, spread the zeolite according to your calculations above. Water it again, then give it a final screed and another water to consolidate the base further.

What turf to buy

The best person to answer this question is a local horticulturalist or greenkeeper. The myriad of turf breeds available all have their strengths and weaknesses. Personally, I like the zoysia breeds, mainly for their finer leaf blade. Saying that, they brown off for a few months during winter and struggle to repair themselves in shadier areas. For warm, humid climates, the soft-leaved buffalo varieties perform quite well, but if I lived in a cool temperate climate, the tall fescues would be my choice. They are so lovely to walk on barefoot.

Top dressing

There is one thing I strongly recommend. When ordering turf from the turf farm, ask them to wash the turf so it's free of the troublesome silty clay that's used to grow it on the farm. It's this 25 mm (1 in) of dark, sticky soil that creates most of the problems.

We've discussed before the perils associated with soil layering and the fact that you could have the best draining soil in the world, but this won't mean a thing while you have a layer of fine silt that bears no resemblance to the soil beneath. Water will have great trouble penetrating the silty band of soil. The grass roots will grow to different depths according to the fluctuating moisture levels. Furthermore, this black silty stuff compacts very easily.

Turf farmers choose to grow the turf on a silty soil to reduce the damage done during the cutting and rolling process. It also helps to hold the rolls together. If you're living on a sandy soil and you're doing the right thing by laying a small lawn, then it may be worthwhile washing or raking the silty soil from the rolls onsite. The silt is rubbish for growing lawn on, but fantastic for amending sandy soils.

Did you know?

The plants growing in a 0.8-hectare (2-acre) wheat field may have more more than 48 280 km (30 000 miles) of roots — that's greater than circumference of the earth.

Once you've laid the washed, soil-less turf, you need to reinstate a soil to replace the silty clay that came from the turf farm. Topdress the turf with the same topsoil you used beneath. This will ensure a uniform soil texture and a better drained lawn that will tolerate compaction and drought with relative ease. Once you've spread and watered in the top dressing, you can give it a gentle roll and then another water to ensure the topsoil has settled around the turf's grass roots.

Make sure your newly laid turf doesn't dry out for the first month or so. Give it frequent light waterings, particularly during the heat of the day. If it's a heatwave and your turf is still establishing, cover it with shade cloth to reduce the impact of stressful conditions.

Mowing

As long as the grass is growing, then continue to mow. If you do it often enough, you'll never have to remove more than 30–40 per cent of the leaf blade. Removing excess leaf area will stress the plants and thus make them less tolerant of drought conditions (see page 80).

Remember, don't scalp your lawn.

LAYING WATER-EFFICIENT TURF

Preparing the turf first is a laborious task, but it's worth it, especially in shady and high-traffic areas as well as areas with no winter sun (otherwise the turf will rot out and compact).

1 Rake the grass side of the turf.

2 Rake the underside.

3 Wash the soil off with a hose.

4 Spread the underlay (80 per cent golf course sand and 20 per cent topsoil with approximately 10 per cent clay content).

5 Add zeolite to the point where you can't see the underlay. About 15–20 per cent of this underlay is zeolite.

6 Add humus or milled compost for water holding. Rake it through, then add granulated chicken manure (one and a half handfuls per square metre/yard will do the trick).

step by step

7 Water in.

8 Unroll the turf. To avoid soil compaction, make sure you use a board to kneel or stand on.

9 Tamp down.

10 Top dress with the same media to avoid incompatibility.

11 Level it up.

12 Wash the top dressing into the turf.

If the grass stops growing due to drought conditions, stop mowing. Slightly raising the mowing height will help reduce some stress on the turf. However, raising the mowing height doesn't mean the plants will use less water, as some people believe. If the lawn receives less than six hours of full sun a day, then set the mower even higher. The more leaf on the turf, the more sunlight it can absorb.

Irrigation

The irrigation chapter (see pages 130–59) gives more detail, but here's a summary of how to have a deep-rooted grass that's tolerant of dry periods.

1 Choose a turf that's suitable for your climate and location. For example, you might live in a warm temperate climate but your garden is in an inland low-lying area that's subject to frost in winter. You need to lay a frost-hardy turf.
2 Only water the turf when it starts to turn a bluish green, a sign that it's suffering from stress.
3 When you do water, check that the soil is evenly drenched to a depth of 15–20 cm (6–8 in).
4 During dry periods, raise the height of the mower blades and also mow less often.
5 Lightly fertilise the turf in summer, especially if you're growing cool-season grasses.

Planting beside driveways and footpaths

Next time you come across a landscape development in a public amenity area, stop and observe the efforts being made to ensure the tree planting's future success. These built environments provide less than hospitable conditions in which trees can establish and mature into landscaping assets. Here are the factors that affect the tree's health and the safety of people in a public area.

A public space needs sealed footpaths and roadways for pedestrian and vehicle traffic as well as trees that provide shade, reduce wind and improve the aesthetics of the space. If people were to walk on soft surfaces such as grass, gravel or consolidated earth, the area would become a dustbowl, the soil would compact and the trees wouldn't mature.

Plan for shade around paved areas so the hard surfaces don't absorb too much heat from the sun.

These problems are solved by hard surfaces. As you know, every action has a reaction associated with it. The hard surfaces protect the soil from millions of feet and tyres, but they also create another set of problems: insufficient infiltration of water and restricted air movement between the soil and atmosphere. (If you need to assert your authority when discussing or debating this topic, use the term 'gaseous exchange' for air movement.)

Gaseous exchange also suffers when soils are compacted. Here's another term to silence the dinner party know-it-all: 'air-filled porosity' reduces more and more as soil compaction increases. Oh yes, and another technical term for you — 'hydraulic conductivity' is the movement of water within the soil.

How tree roots grow

Now you know what effect your actions can have on the welfare of the tree. Let's look at what detrimental effects the tree's actions can have upon you. 'Pardon me?' you say. Trees have amazing power and strength and are also blessed with patience and time. Trees fully understand that without water, they're doomed. Their ability to plan forward is a shining example that our politicians could learn from.

Let me explain. While there are nutrients and water within the tree's feeding zone, it will happily grow flowers, leaves and branches upstairs and roots downstairs. It will also invest energy into producing explorative roots. These roots will keep growing without increasing their girth, as they don't need to. Yet. The tree is quite prepared to accept that some, if not many, roots will meet a Scott of the Antarctic fate in return for perhaps only one becoming the Marco Polo root.

So this successful explorer, which is probably no thicker than string, finds 'pay dirt'. On its journey of 5, 10, 20 or more metres or yards, it will come across soil conditions that possess the right stuff for growth. Once our exploring root starts absorbing the water and nutrients, its ability to divide cells is fuelled by two sources: the tree as well as the pot of gold it has just found. Messages are sent back to the tree via chemicals called auxins, informing the tree of the exciting news. At this point, things happen very quickly. The girth of our wee exploring root thickens quite rapidly in order to increase the movement of resources. The tip of the exploring root branches exponentially. Depending on the species of tree, this root could increase in size by 1000 per cent within the growing season.

Now, consider what happens to built structures when something that's the thickness of string gradually increases to the thickness of an elephant's trunk. Stuff moves! Built stuff, such as concrete slabs, drainage pipes, retaining walls and building foundations.

So in a landscape development, if you provide ideal growing conditions for the tree's survival but not enough for the tree's needs when it matures,

FERTILISING JACARANDA

Even a mature tree can benefit from fertilising.

1 This mature jacaranda on the edge of a lawn could do with some extra nutrients.

2 Make some holes in the turf about 60 cm (24 in) apart and 1–2 m (3–4 ft) from the trunk, but within the tree's drip line.

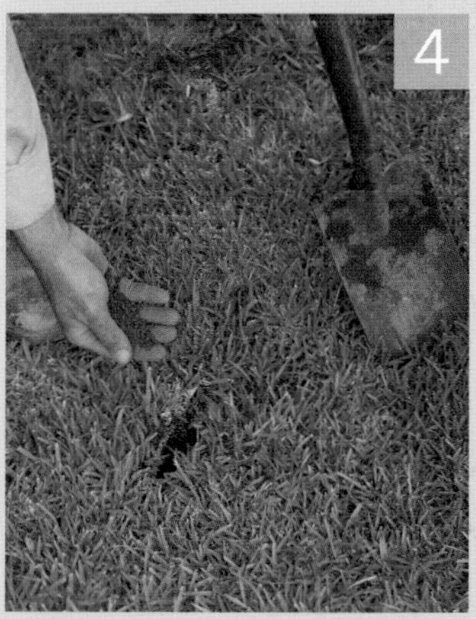

3 We used granulated chicken manure for this job.

4 Insert the manure in the holes you've made.

it will go looking for these conditions itself. Next time you trip over or stub your toe on an uneven, cracked or uplifted pathway, you've just been reminded that someone didn't do their job properly.

Now, I need to clarify something in case you think I'm contradicting myself. Elsewhere I've stated that roots won't grow into dry or inhospitable soil. The point of difference I'm trying to make comes down to one letter: *roots* won't grow into hostile soils but a *root* sometimes will.

The ornamental fig species (or Port Jackson fig, *Ficus rubiginosa*) provides brilliant examples of this kind of root behaviour. To watch it in progress gives me such a thrill. Many figs rely on birds and bats to spread their seed. Many germinate in the boughs of trees or perhaps in a crack in the side of a rock face. The seedling will pop out one or two leaves and that's all it needs and all it can afford for the time being. These two leaves are the wee solar panels for a lonely explorer root that grows down the trunk of the tree or rock face, slowly, perhaps only a few centimetres each season in dry times, or metres in ideal conditions, to find a source of water and nutrients. (This process is called geotropism, where the roots sense gravitational pull and grow downwards.) Once the explorer root touches the soil (providing it's moist enough) — whammo! It's time for action.

How do we address the tree's needs while protecting the built structure from its bionic strength? And what on earth has this got to do with planting around residential hard surfaces? Plenty! You need to look at how the big budget projects successfully grow and sustain healthy mature trees so you can adapt their practices to your limited budget or planting project. The cost of achieving healthy plants beside hard surfaces isn't that significant, especially when you compare it to the physical costs of possibly removing a dead 7-year-old tree and/or the cost or disappointment of your failed plan. Remember, we smart gardeners leave nothing to chance.

Let's look at the effects a slab of impervious material has on the soil beneath and around it.

1. The soil beneath a slab will have insufficient gaseous exchange for encouraging root growth. In other words, our desired 25 per cent of air in the soil is more like 2.5 per cent.
2. There's probably plenty of moisture beneath, but thanks to the minimal air-filled porosity within the soil, the moisture and nutrients have turned anaerobic and, as such, it's become a bit of a no-go zone for most species, with the exception of bog or swamp-loving plants such as willows (*Salix* sp.) and poplars (*Populus* sp.). Any roots that venture under the slab usually occupy the uppermost part of the soil directly beneath the bottom of the slab. If the root happens to increase in girth size, something has to give, and that's usually the concrete slab or paving.
3. During wet weather, the hard-surface water runoff creates erosion, leaches the soils and, in low areas, inundates the plants with Noah's ark conditions. Without fail, it deposits excess soil over the existing plant's root zones, resulting in slow suffocation or smelly cases of root or collar rot disease.

Aerial roots growing on a cliff face.

4 The additional reflective heat and light from the built structure increase evaporation from the surrounding soil and transpiration rates in plants. These conditions can also lead to significant leaf and bark scorch damage during heatwave conditions.
5 When plants experience these stressful conditions, they're prone to attack by pests and disease.

Laying a concrete slab

It's not hard to reverse these conditions into something plants like and, at the same time, protect the hard surface from future structural damage. Simply prepare the ground beneath the slab. It takes a little thought and, in cases where structural integrity is important, you may need to engage an engineer to design or consult on the construction methods. If your builder or landscaper is planning to pour a concrete slab, then have a chat to them about providing the following conditions beneath the surface. Not only will your garden benefit, so too will the contractor's knowledge. Hopefully in the future they'll use this approach on other projects, ensuring long-term success.

Step 1

To ensure the hard surface doesn't settle or sink, it's important that the entire slab hasn't been poured on a completely cultivated area. Certain areas of the slab must be in contact with properly consolidated ground. Chat to the builder about the appropriate distances between these piers or foundation zones. Once these have been marked out, make sure the ground has been cultivated to eliminate compaction (as discussed on page 35). Mix a small amount of compost with slow-release fertiliser into the prepared ground.

Step 2

Trench and lay slotted PVC drainage pipe into the prepared soil. If the surface is not level, then trench these pipes perpendicular to the fall of the land. Space them approximately 1.5 m (5 ft) apart and leave them exposed at both ends. These pipes will act as service conduits to the soil beneath the hard surface and will:

- allow air movement between the atmosphere and soil beneath the hard surface;
- reduce anaerobic conditions within the soil;
- provide access for water and nutrients;
- allow waterlogged conditions to dry out;
- greatly reduce concentrated surface water runoff by directing water to drain beneath the slab, not beside it; and
- provide water infiltration zones that will increase groundwater recharging.

These improved conditions will encourage the adjacent plants to take advantage of the additional growing area and so improve their health and strength as well as their opportunity to achieve their mature size and shape.

One further benefit of this practice is that, should future contractors need to move pipes, wires or cables from one side of the slab to the other, they'll be able to do so with ease. They can simply feed it through one of the PVC pipes. This could save you a lot of money down the track.

Lombardy poplar (*Populus nigra* 'Italica').

TOP AND ABOVE Segmented paving over a structural soil is great for street planting and driveways because it holds moisture and allows the air to get in.

OPPOSITE In this paved tropical courtyard garden, the plantings have been used to create a feeling of depth.

Converting impervious paving to porous paving

Porous paving is designed to allow air and water to pass through. At the moment it comprises just a small fraction of all pavement installations. However, its popularity is steadily increasing throughout the world.

Most hard surfaces around homes provide hostile growing conditions but, perversely, home gardeners are often advised to surround these 'solar reflectors' or 'water repellers' with lots of green stuff so the area will feel cooler, look nicer and be more inviting to utilise. Later on, in 'Smart gardening' (pages 164–87), we discuss the adverse effects hard surfaces have on the surrounding growing areas. Here are the main points to note.

1 Reflective heat from the surface increases soil evaporation and plants' transpiration.
2 A rapid inundation of water, due to surface runoff, results in such problems as waterlogged soil, erosion and nutrient leaching.
3 Within water runoff there are increased levels of pollutants, such as cleaning products, automobile oils, and salts or chlorine from pools entering stormwater systems and surrounding soils.
4 There's no opportunity for gaseous exchange or infiltration of water into the soil beneath the hard surface.
5 There is reduced soil volume for healthy root growth.

I often shake my head in wonder when I see council-approved building developments going on beneath mature trees. Laying a sealed driveway or a patio over the root zone of a mature tree sentences the tree to a 'death of a thousand cuts'. Slowly (or, in some cases, rapidly), the tree loses condition, becomes susceptible to pests and diseases, drops large branches or, in strong winds, falls over. Why? Because the many roots that have been ensuring the tree's survival have been rendered useless by suffocation and dehydration.

It's also worth keeping in mind that trees take a long time to grow, so quite often they take a long time to die.

Once again, the solution is relatively simple and, if you like using power tools, the task is quite exciting.

INJECTING NUTRIENTS

The following treatment will increase the root zone and reduce stormwater runoff, and next spring, growth will take off.

1 This Tahitian lime, planted between the house wall and the concrete driveway, looks malnourished and distressed.

2 Drill holes in the concrete.

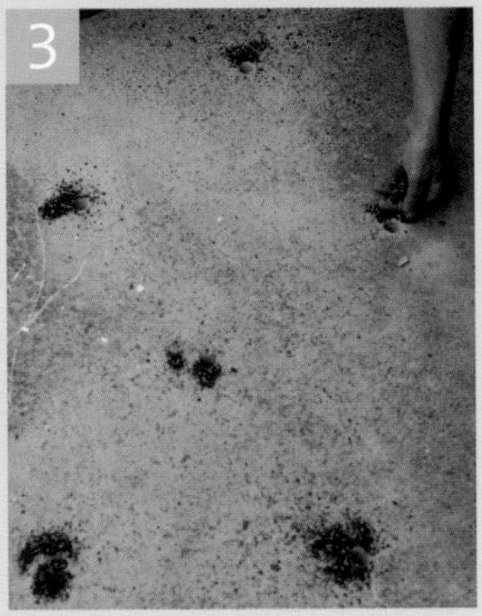

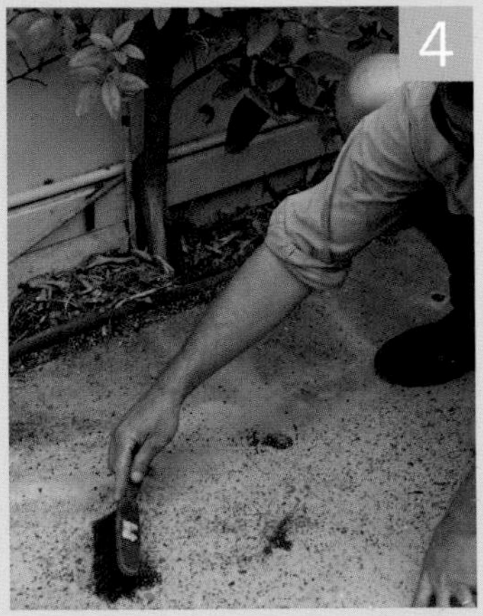

3 Into the holes insert a mix of 80 per cent chicken manure and 20 per cent six months controlled-release fertiliser.

4 Brush in any excess, then water in.

Injecting nutrients around trees

Have a look at the Tahitian limes in the photo at left. They've been planted between the house and driveway for a couple of reasons. The first and most obvious reason is for fruit. They also provide a cooling effect by shading the wall of the house. The third reason is aesthetic.

Since planting, the limes' needs for healthy growth have been met. However, each year, as the trees have grown, their needs for more resources have also grown. Judging by the yellowing leaves and pests taking up residence, the lime trees are not receiving the resources they need.

The solution is to create favourable conditions beneath the concrete driveway. By drilling small (20 mm) holes through the concrete to access the soil beneath, you'll ensure the delivery of nutrients, water and oxygen to the dormant soil beneath. Once you've drilled the holes, nature will do the rest. The soil will awaken and the roots will venture in and exploit the area. Provided the holes are spaced no closer than 45 cm (18 in) and are drilled in a staggered pattern, the concrete slab and trees will live together happily ever after. As time goes on, the trees may start to show signs of distress again. At that time, you may need to clear the holes of blockages or even drill more holes.

Creating access through a layer of sand

Converting impervious surfaces into permeable paving is relatively simple when you're dealing with concrete. But what if you need to create access through paving bricks or flagstones, where there's a layer of sand between the concrete base slab and the paving surface? This requires a little more consideration and effort.

Future problems can arise when the sand between the pavers and the concrete starts to erode into the holes. The sand won't bother the feeder roots beneath, but it will make the pavers subside and possibly create a pedestrian hazard.

The answer is pretty simple. First, go to the hardware store and buy some electrical conduit

Laying gravel in an outdoor eating area allows rainwater to soak through into the soil below.

that complements the drill size you're using. I find 20 mm conduit (plastic pipe) fits nicely into 20 mm drill holes, especially after a few taps with a rubber mallet or a lump of timber. Don't use a metal hammer, or the useful piece of pipe will turn into many pieces of useless plastic.

If you're drilling through concrete, follow the steps above, but before you pour anything into the holes, measure the depth of your drill hole. Use a depth gauge or lower a screwdriver or something straight into the hole until it hits the soil beneath. Cut the conduit according to the depth required and pop it in the hole. It may take extra time but it's best to drill and install the conduit one hole at a time, otherwise the vibrations from the next hole you drill will encourage the sand to fall into the previous hole, resulting in a depression in the paving surface.

To secure loose-fitting pipe, smear a splodge of construction adhesive around the outside of the pipe. The nutrients you add to each hole depend on the plant species. For citrus and roses, I like to add 20 per cent slow-release fertiliser and 80 per cent composted chicken manure, but if I'm liberating trees and shrubs, I use cow manure instead of chicken.

The benefits of converting to porous paving go beyond improving your microclimate. The water that is diverted from the stormwater system and back into the ground increases the quantity of water that is able to slowly infiltrate the small creeks and streams, providing water reserves for street trees and other plantings. The surplus water from this infiltration will slowly make its way down to the depths of your groundwater supplies.

Tips for young players

If you're fired up about reducing your contribution to stormwater pollutants and at the same time giving the water table a much needed top-up, then engage a

hydraulics engineer to advise you on the most effective ways to adapt your home to help infiltration. Otherwise, follow this advice.

- If you're unsure of the hard surface, hire a structural engineer to inspect the slab.
- Before you start drilling, consider what may be beneath the hard surface you're about to work on. Identify and locate possible hazards such as electricity, mains water or drainage lines. If in doubt, engage a 'services locating contractor' to scan the area with their magic locating machine.
- Always use an earth leakage safety switch with the drill. You don't want to electrocute yourself.
- Wear the appropriate personal protective equipment, such as a dust mask, and goggles and earmuffs to protect your eyes and ears when you're drilling and cleaning out the dust and debris.
- Be aware that stone in concrete can explode and expel chips into your face.
- Percussion or hammer drills are designed to work at their own pace. The operator's job is to hold the machine steady so the drill remains in contact with the impact zone. Lifting the drill up slightly then down again every 30 seconds or so helps to clear the concrete dust from the impact zone.
- If you're drilling pilot holes first, ensure the diameter of the pilot drill bit is less than a quarter of the final drill size. For example, a 20-mm final hole size requires a pilot drill of 5 mm or less.
- The older the concrete, the harder it will be to drill.
- When the drill is part of the way through the concrete, reduce the drill speed. This will provide you with approximately 3 seconds prior warning of the drill breaking through. As soon as you're through, hold the drill steady at the 'breakthrough' depth. Pull the trigger a couple of times and reverse the drill out. This method will ensure that, should there be any services beneath, the drill won't puncture them.
- Don't attempt the task with a home handyman hammer drill. It will take you a month of Sundays to complete, the drill will probably self-destruct and you will need a second mortgage to pay for the numerous drill bits you'll need.
- Borrow or hire a construction standard percussion drill like the one I'm using in photo 2 on page 122. The job will take four hours instead of a whole back-breaking weekend.

If it all sounds too involved, hire a concrete-cutting contractor, landscaper or builder, and let them do all the hard slog.

OPPOSITE The informal plantings edging this flight of stairs contrast with the formal clipped edge and focal point beyond.

5

Irrigation

Irrigation

A drip irrigation system, ideally in combination with a rainwater tank system, will help to conserve water in times of drought.

Regardless of what type of garden you have, eventually you'll need to provide it with some water. So although the purpose of this book is to help you devise and care for a garden that relies mainly on rainfall, you'll still need to prepare for those times when mother nature fails to come to the party.

Saving water

Irrigation manufacturers promote their systems as efficient ways to help save the planet's water, but this claim is only true when the systems are installed and managed correctly. In my experience, only a small proportion of the systems installed are entitled to boast about their capacity to save water.

Fact: irrigation systems make life easier because you don't need to spend time watering. Fact: if you don't need to spend time watering, you won't notice how much overwatering the system is doing. Here's a tip. If you own a system, turn it off now, then count the days until your garden looks as if it really needs water. You'll probably find that your garden will survive quite well with half the quantity of water you're currently providing.

Now here's the important part. If you want to do the right thing and reduce the quantity of water you're providing your garden with, don't reduce the time period that your system is set for. Instead, extend the period *between* watering days. You may find your system is set to use 2000 L (440 gall) twice a week during summer. If you can tweak it back to half that amount, you could save a whopping 60 000 L (13 200 gall) a year.

So there you have it. Irrigate deeply at long intervals rather than give plants frequent, shallow waterings. Deep watering improves drought resistance by promoting deeper, more extensive root systems. Remember that roots are opportunistic. They can grow towards areas that provide the two most important things they need for survival: water and air. In areas where dry summers are normal, most woody plants with extensive root systems can survive on only half the water they would otherwise transpire.

If you have the money, engage the services of a competent irrigation technician and a knowledgeable horticulturalist. They'll accurately determine your garden's water requirements, recommend a suitable irrigation system and also properly audit and calibrate it.

Changing community attitudes

At some time or another, most communities have experienced water restrictions. Draconian ones were imposed on my hometown in 2003 and they're still in place today. Sadly, the restrictions are due more to lack of forward planning and a failure to invest in our region's future than to lack of rainfall.

During a drought, many large companies profit from primary and secondary resource exploitation. Together with those private garden owners who can afford it, they've drilled bores to maintain their lust for excessive water use. It's disappointing: cash is applied to the problem when what's needed is a long-term solution that

PREVIOUS SPREAD AND OPPOSITE This rainforest garden isn't part of a national park. It's on a large suburban block in a warm temperate climate that's experienced drought for several years. It hasn't been watered — except by rain — for the last four years.

might lead to some change in community attitudes. For example, wouldn't it be appropriate to reserve groundwater for the benefit of the greater community by only using it on sports fields and botanic gardens? Anyway, that's my beef on the way the world's heading.

If, like me, you can only dream of becoming a benevolent millionaire, then you'll have to make do with what mother nature provides and sleep well with the thought that you're challenging yourself and your garden to perform without a constant dribble of water to keep it unsustainably green.

A vital first step towards caring for the environment is to change your current attitude towards irrigation. Irrigation should be supplementary, not necessary. It's not a crime to use water in your garden, but it is wrong to *overuse* water in your garden. That's why I've deliberately kept this chapter to the basics. We should all be trying to rely on rainfall for garden watering. By rainfall I mean on- and offsite rainwater harvesting and large-scale waste water and stormwater recycling, so that we only use water from the sustainable section of the water cycle.

Infiltration and water penetration

Before we get onto the nuts and bolts of irrigation, we need to know a bit about how soil absorbs water.

Infiltration refers to the amount of water that passes through the soil surface in terms of depth (centimetres or inches) in a given time period (usually one hour).

Providing the soil isn't sunbaked and repelling water, lighter textured soils, such as sands or sandy loams, have much faster infiltration rates — that is, water will penetrate into the soil relatively quickly so that no runoff or puddling occurs. Heavy-textured soils, such as clay, often have slower rates of water penetration or infiltration, because the space that the soil occupies is relatively dense. Adding organic matter facilitates infiltration by opening up the soil — something we covered in detail in 'Amending the soil' (pages 30–51).

OPPOSITE You can achieve striking effects with colour and form in a succulent garden.

Why install an irrigation system?

If you water the soil with a sprinkler or hose, you're filling the soil to capacity with water and delivering water to the soil more quickly than it can cope with. This results in runoff, which removes nutrients and topsoil from the landscape. Conversely, your conscious efforts to reduce water consumption may oblige you to race around your garden watering a little bit everywhere, resulting in your plants maintaining shallow root systems.

You might then leave the soil to completely dry out and only when the plants are showing signs of severe stress do you give the garden a huge 'guilt drink' in the hope that it'll do the trick. Once again, you saturate the soil, pushing the oxygen out of it. This is a lose/lose situation for your garden.

Drip irrigation keeps the water and oxygen levels within sustainable limits. If you plan never to have any system and instead rely on the garden hose, then your best approach is to turn the tap on ever so slightly, just until a small trickle of water exits the hose pipe. Measure the amount of water dribbling out and place the hose within the root zone or garden bed (preferably at the highest point of either of these in order to exploit gravity). Leave it there until it delivers 40 L (9 gall), then shift it a metre or so to the next dry spot.

This method is very effective when you're working in the garden, as you can easily monitor the amount of water your plants are getting.

Here are the practical implications of infiltration rates of soils on irrigation.

1 All soils will take up water rapidly at first, until the first 12 mm (1/2 in) becomes wet, then slow down in water uptake.
2 Soils with faster infiltration rates need to be irrigated more frequently in order to meet the plant's water requirements.
3 Soils with slow infiltration rates should be watered in 'shifts' or cycles so that the water can soak in.

The soil type also has a lot to do with how deep water penetrates into the soil. Where there are soils with large particle sizes (sands/sandy loams), or soils with good aggregation, water will penetrate the soil more deeply than if the soil is poorly structured and has large amounts of smaller particles, such as in clays and silts.

On a typical sandy loam soil, 25 mm (1 in) of water may penetrate to a depth of 30 cm (12 in). A 'clay' soil may have the same 25 mm (1 in) of water penetrate to only 10 cm (4 in). A 'loam' soil would be intermediate. Why? Loam contains about 60 per cent sand, and up to about 30 per cent silt and 15 per cent clay. The depth of water penetration is also dependent on how wet the soil is at the time of watering or rainfall. The wetter the soil, the deeper the water will go. Remember that sand allows water to drain freely, holding and absorbing very little, while silt and clays have the ability to absorb and hold water for longer periods. This also explains why there's a difference in the depth of penetration.

Inheriting an irrigation system

Let me paint the common scenario. You've just moved into a home that boasts a fully automated irrigation system. Cash is tight and, if you're like me, you're itching to check out the system. (It's interesting to note that males remain fascinated by hoses and water throughout their lives. I'm sure that right about now, I've lost 99 per cent of female readers to another chapter.)

First, let me say these futile words: *if you're not familiar with irrigation systems, leave them alone!* Right, my duty of care is now complete. You can go and fiddle with the timer. Once you're totally confused, carefully put the thing back together, call an irrigation technician and pretend you never touched it.

When properly tuned and programmed, irrigation systems save water and time and improve the growing conditions and as such, the yield of plants. Unfortunately, most domestic systems are poorly designed and installed haphazardly. Under these circumstances, irrigation is dreadfully wasteful. The info below should hopefully save you the cost of hiring an irrigation technician.

Check the equipment

Check that the system installed is appropriate for your garden. For example, rotor heads are good for watering large areas of turf but spray heads deliver water in a third of the time. If you have rotor heads, set the timer

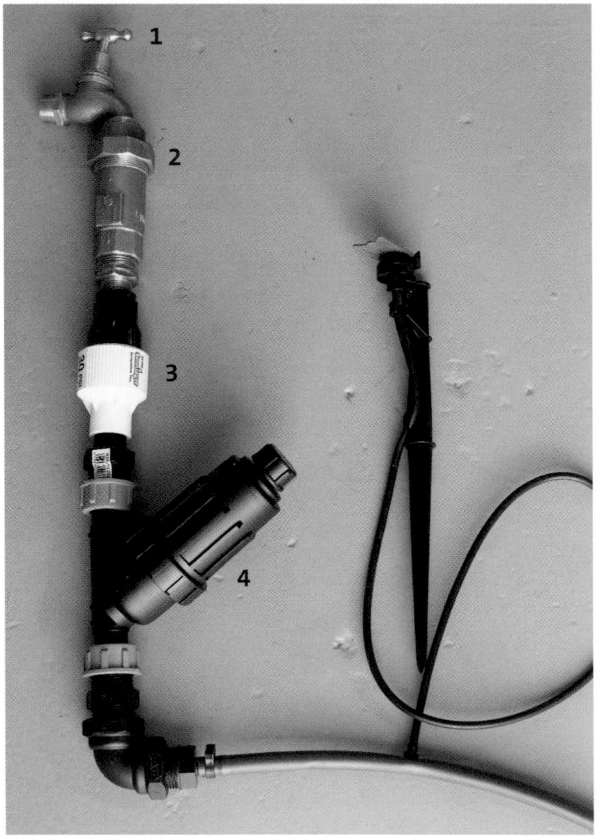

Some components of an irrigation system: a tap (1), backflow control valve (2), pressure limiting valve (3) and filter (4).

to deliver water for three times as long as you would a spray head. All the heads in one zone should be of the same type.

Make sure your irrigation system meets code regulations and has backflow preventers to protect your family's safety.

If your garden has slopes, water will run off unless you've installed swales and soakaways at strategic points (see page 21). Use nozzles with a slow delivery rate on slopes. If your irrigation control box has a cycle and soak program, this is the time to use it. This program allows the system to deliver water intermittently, providing the soil with enough time to absorb the water before runoff occurs.

Evaluate the coverage

Are any parts of the garden left completely dry or too wet? This may be due to a number of factors, as shown in the table below.

Calculating your sprinkler's precipitation rate

Before we start, I'd better demystify this term. The precipitation rate is the quantity of water (in millimetres

You can calculate your sprinkler's precipitation rate by measuring the amount of water in a number of jars or cans of the same size.

FACTORS AFFECTING COVERAGE

Soil is too dry	Soil is too wet
The heads have been installed too far apart or in the wrong pattern	Water naturally collects at the lowest point in the landscape
The water pressure is low	Shady areas are over-irrigated
The nozzle is blocked	A leaky valve is causing constant seepage: either replace the whole valve or the worn diaphragms in the solenoid valves
The site is exposed to wind and sun (easterly in the northern hemisphere and westerly in the southern hemisphere). This area may need up to twice as much water as a shady, protected site	

step by step

REGULATING THE FLOW

Too much water? You need to regulate the flow.

This weeping hose system is fitted with in-line taps, a type of adjustable dripper that's one of my favourites. Having emitters on their own flexible tubes means you can accurately deliver the water where it's needed as well as adjust the quantity of water.

1 To reduce the flow rate, turn down the tap. I've screwed the emitter head clockwise to the point of being virtually shut off so it emits only 2 L (3 1/2 pt) per hour.

2 Now I've turned it fully counterclockwise. At this setting the emitter is delivering a staggering 288 L (63 gall) per hour.

3 If you carry on turning it counterclockwise, the emitter head will detach itself from the stake and tube. This feature is handy for clearing blockages from the line.

or inches) that lands on the sprinkler's wetting area in a given amount of time. This calculation is reasonably simple.

1. Place 5–6 straight-edged food cans or jars of the same size in one zone of the irrigation system or around the lawn sprinkler. *Note*: The more cans you use, the more accurate the test.
2. Turn on the zone or sprinkler and run it for a set period of time — say, 30 minutes.
3. Use a ruler to measure the depth of water in each can and record it.
4. Calculate the average depth of water from all the cans.
5. Repeat this sequence for all zones.

Example

Say five cans were used for zone 1 in the irrigation system. The amount of water found in the five cans was as follows: 127, 102, 152, 102 and 152 mm (0.5, 0.4, 0.6, 0.4 and 0.6 in). Add the depths together and you'll get 6.35 cm (2.5 in) of water.

Divide this figure by 5 (cans) = 1.27 cm (1/2 in) of water in 30 minutes or 25 mm (1 in) of water per hour. This means that to apply the necessary amount of supplemental irrigation for healthy plant growth, zone 1 would need to be run for one hour each week in spring and autumn, and for about 1.5–1.75 hours in the heat of summer.

Soaker hoses or drip irrigation

If you're using soaker hoses or drip irrigation, it's not so easy to determine how much water is being applied. There will always be more water in the soil closer to the hose or to each emitter than at a distance. Check a few spots in the irrigated area by carefully digging out the soil with a trowel or spade. Ideally, you should apply enough water so that the top 15 cm (6 in) is moist, but not soggy, a few hours after the irrigation system has been turned off. If water starts to run off before the areas are thoroughly soaked, turn off the sprinklers or hoses and don't turn them on again until the soil becomes more absorbent.

ABOVE Water meter.

RIGHT *Salvia* 'Indigo Spires'.

To calculate how much water you're using, you can check the water meter.

Reading from the far right, the meter will count litres, then tens of litres, then hundreds of litres, and so on.

1. Ensure that no other taps are running.
2. Turn on the tap that's feeding the system so that it emits its usual quantity.
3. Watch the meter, focusing on the numbers at the right-hand side of the counter. If they're zipping around at a frantic speed then the far right digits are counting litres. I say this because some meters have tens of litres as the lowest digits.
4. When the right-hand counter passes 0, count for 10 seconds. When the 10 seconds is up, write down the number on the meter. If it's only just made it to the next digit number, then you're definitely working with tens of litres.

handy hint

If possible, don't use overhead sprinklers for shrub and flower beds. It's best to either hand water or use drip or trickle irrigation. Greater water loss can occur with overhead irrigation because of evaporation and wind drift.

CLEANING OUT A LOW-PRESSURE FILTER

1 Unscrew the cap and remove the filter.

2 Hose it out.

3 Screw it back on.

For this exercise, let's say the meter counted 5 L (9 pt) of water passing through in the 10 seconds.

1 To determine how much you're using every minute, multiply 5 L x 6 (10-second increments) = 30 L (7 gall) per minute.

2 Taking the next step to determine the hourly consumption rate is much the same. Multiply the 30 L per minute x 60 (minutes in the hour) and that comes to 1800 L (396 gall) per hour.

In this way, you can calculate how much water each water-using appliance uses in your home. Once you've gathered the information on the consumption rates of appliances — especially how long your teenager spends in the shower — you can properly start to challenge your current water usage.

Regular maintenance

Make sure you regularly check any sections of the system that are missing their mark — for example, check the spray heads and lines for any leaks or clogs. And remember, you shouldn't mix bubblers, drip emitters and lawn sprinklers in the same automatic zone. Irrigation companies, garden stores or other professionals can provide you with valuable advice.

Drip irrigation system

If you're starting your garden from scratch, I recommend you install a drip irrigation system — the most efficient way to supplement rainfall. This sort of system slowly waters the soil immediately above or below the surface of the soil. The water flows under low pressure through plastic pipe or hose, which has been strategically laid among the plants, and oozes into the soil through tiny holes called orifices. These orifices are either inserted by you or factory-fitted along the hose at regular intervals or in fittings called emitters, which are plugged into the hose at the desired spacing.

Drip irrigation is ideal for vegetables, ornamental and fruit trees, shrubs, vines and container-grown plants outdoors but not so suitable for plantings of shallow-rooted plants, such as lawns and some groundcovers.

Under lawns, it can be difficult to determine consistent flow rates of water. As most contractors provide minimum ground preparation for turf, the drip system often floods the subsoil. Without chemical control, the tiny root hairs invade and block the drip emitters. If you're relieving compacted soil within a lawn, you will puncture the hoses.

Troubles also arise when grass roots enter the drip emitters and block them. Manufacturers of drip irrigation systems have addressed this problem by providing a steady supply of a herbicide called trifluralin in the system to inhibit all root growth around the drip emitter.

There is very little information available on the effects of exposure to this poison. Studies have shown that it's moderately toxic to rats and mice after a very short period of exposure to the stuff. The United States Environmental Protection Agency has determined that it's quite likely to cause cancer in humans and has the potential to leach into groundwater supplies.

Typically, the manufacturers and industries endorsing this chemical for safe use in drip systems happen to have a financial interest in selling the product. Feel free to make your own decision on whether it's good or bad. Me? I don't design gardens with unsuitably large lawns, thus avoiding the need to spend time and money on a wasteful exercise.

Advantages of drip irrigation

The real value to your garden of using drip irrigation is that the amount of moisture in the soil remains relatively constant and air — just as essential to the plant root system as water — is always available. But there are several other excellent reasons why you should install a drip irrigation system.

FIXING A NICK IN THE IRRIGATION LINE

1 A nick in the irrigation line wastes water. Run the tap to find it.

2 Cut the line.

3 Insert the tube in one end and a clip on each side of the cut.

4 Push them together and move the clips onto the join. Use a tool to get them on if necessary.

ABOVE In raised garden beds, you'll need weep holes so the water can drain away.

OPPOSITE Ornamental grasses like this fountain grass (*Pennisetum* sp.) are native to warm temperate and tropical climates.

- The amount of water lost to evaporation, runoff and evapotranspiration is reduced by 60 per cent or more.
- Plants are protected from extreme fluctuations in temperature.
- Water soaks in immediately and is accessible to plant roots.
- Wind won't carry water away as it does with sprinkler systems.
- There's no overspray, which can result in staining and mould spots on fences and house sidings.
- The low volume requirements of drip irrigation are ideal for old galvanised steel water service lines that have become corroded and narrow.
- The irrigation zones can be constantly adjusted by repositioning, adding or removing emitter lines and emitters.

handy hint

To further reduce water consumption, plug drip lines when plants are removed or die.

Disadvantages of drip irrigation

The few cons associated with this type of system can be overcome. If you don't have the correct number of emitters, or they're poorly placed, it can be difficult to see if the system is working properly. This is where you need to take the time to fine tune the system to suit your garden's needs. If your drip system requires you to physically turn the water on and off, or if the controller is faulty, the system could remain operating indefinitely. You can get around this by installing an indicator device where a little flag pops up when the water is flowing.

Another problem is that the tubing can be a hazard if it's not laid properly. Just secure it with anchor pins every metre (3 ft) or so, and cover it with mulch.

Did you know?

A single tree can provide the same cooling effect as ten room-sized air-conditioners working 24 hours a day. For example, a willow tree transpires 19 000 L (5000 gall) of water a day.

Anchor your irrigation lines at regular intervals, otherwise they'll create a hazard.

Salinity from groundwater

When we pump water from underground, we often bring dissolved salts and minerals to the surface with it. If we splash this type of water around our plants willy nilly and allow plenty of it to evaporate into the atmosphere, it won't be too long before the elements left behind accumulate in the topsoil. Soil salinity is land degradation and that's a place we don't want to be. If you're gardening and find that you're degrading the soil you're gardening with, then it's time to go back to 'Amending the soil'.

Salts also reduce the amount of water available to plants. If you have poor quality water containing a moderate amount of salts, using a drip irrigation system will add less salt because less water is applied. Also, the higher and more uniform level of soil moisture helps to keep the salt concentration at a lower level in the soil. In periods of low rainfall, apply additional irrigation to help leach the salts from the soil. A good time to do this is when the plants need less water.

Installing a drip irrigation system

These days water is extremely precious, and it's becoming more expensive as governments try to encourage us to use less by raising the cost of town water. We should all be trying to make the most of every precious drop of this life-sustaining resource. If you've previously shied away from installing a drip irrigation system because it seemed too complicated or expensive, don't worry — I'll explain why it's both easy and economical. And don't forget that, over time, the savings you make in water costs will help pay for the system.

How much you spend on irrigation depends on whether you want a simple system or one with all the bells and whistles, such as automatic controls (great if you lead a very busy life and are often away from home), pressure regulators and fertiliser injectors. My advice is to keep it simple, and consider your needs one at a time.

Water source

You're going to need a source of clean water that flows at a rate of at least 7.5–18 L (2–5 gall) per minute with at least 14–18 kpa (30–40 lb) water pressure, otherwise sand, silt and other debris may clog up the emitters. If you're using town water you probably don't require a filter, but it's a good idea to add one just in case.

Filtration system

Choose your filtration system according to the type and quantity of foreign materials in the water and/or emitter characteristics. On the whole, though, I reckon a screen-type filter is best. Since we're keeping it simple, use a filter system on the main line near the main water supply rather than install several throughout the irrigation system.

Types of filters

There are a couple of different types of filters. Y-type filters have in-line strainers containing single, 100-mesh, corrosion-resistant stainless steel or bronze screens. These are usually fine for filtering small quantities of sand and other particles.

On the other hand, if your water supply contains larger amounts of sand, you'll need filters with replaceable cartridges, synthetic fibre fabric elements or multi-stage screens, such as 100- and 180-mesh.

Make sure your filters are equipped with cleanout or flush valves so you can easily remove trapped particles. In areas where water contains moderate amounts of sand and other materials, you'll need to flush the filter daily.

handy hint

A decrease in water pressure and volume delivered can signal filter clogging, while a decrease in flow, in spite of good pressure in the lines, indicates emitter clogging.

Planning the system

The simplest way to start out is to make a sketch of the area to be irrigated on grid or graph paper. Using a scale of 1 cm/inch = 1 metre/yard will make the maths so much easier. I always trace the garden plan onto tracing paper, then pop graph paper underneath the tracing paper to measure out the quantity of material I'll need.

Keep in mind that each irrigation zone should be no more than 30 m (33 yd) away from a tap. Beyond that distance, the volume of running water decreases to such a low level that the drip system may not run properly in a large area.

Draw in the length of 2-cm (3/4-in) or 13-mm (1/2-in) hose or plastic pipe needed to connect the irrigation system to the tap, then measure it. Usually a 13-mm hose is a sufficient line size for a domestic garden.

I won't tell you how to lay out the system, as this will depend on the type of garden area you're irrigating, the system you're installing and your topography. For

step by step

CLEANING OUT A HIGH-PRESSURE FILTER

Cleaning the filter on a high-pressure system is simply a matter of holding the filter under running water.

1 Remove the filter, which is a series of mesh discs.

2 Wash it under running water.

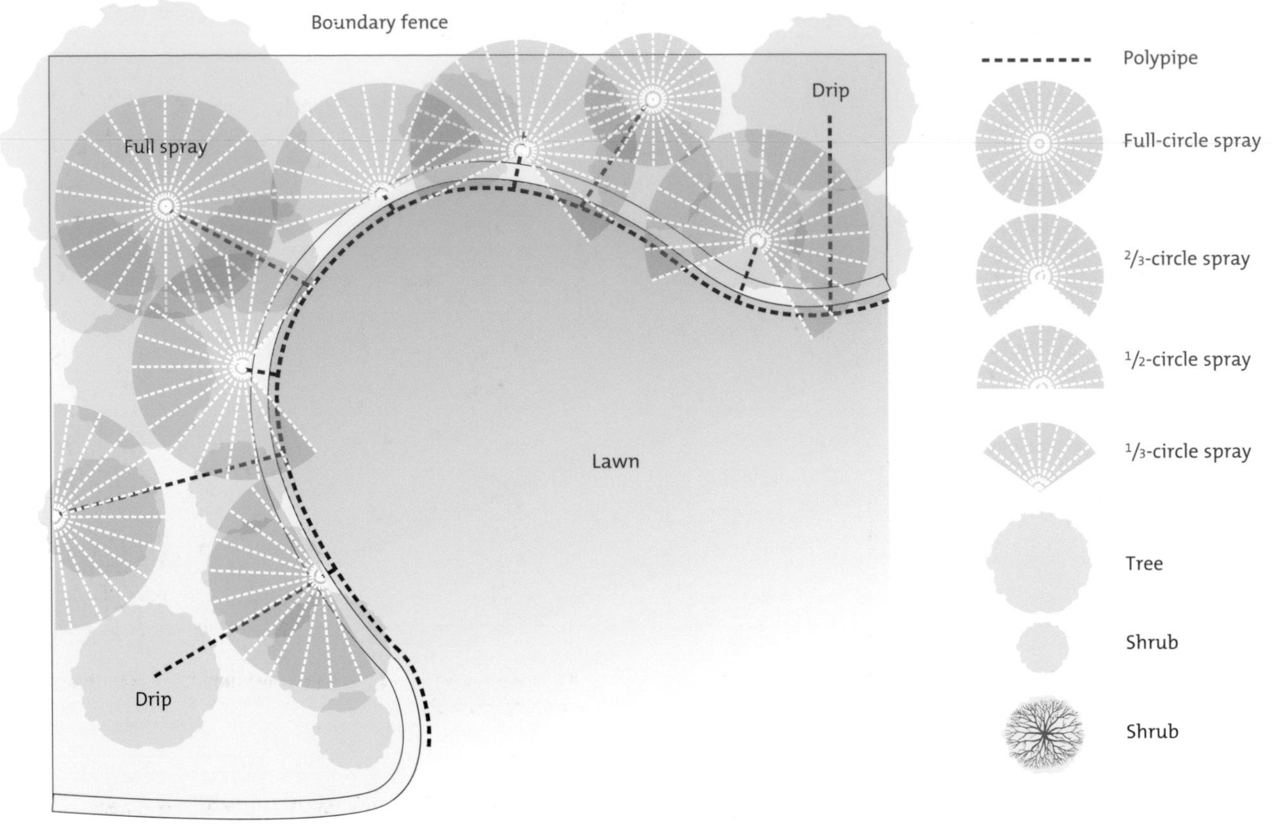
Boundary fence
Full spray
Drip
Lawn
Drip
Polypipe
Full-circle spray
2/3-circle spray
1/2-circle spray
1/3-circle spray
Tree
Shrub
Shrub

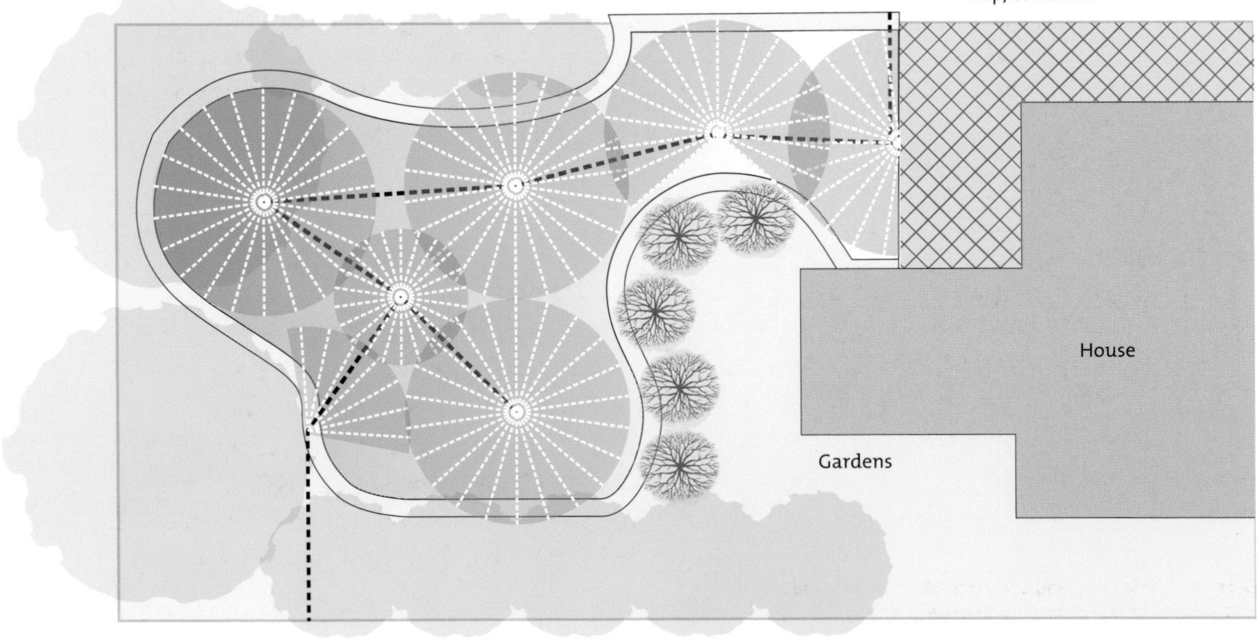
Tap/controller
House
Gardens

Handwatering wastes water — it's far more efficient to water the roots with an irrigation system.

Now that the irrigation lines have been installed, this bed is ready for planting and mulching.

example, for a vegetable garden you might be looking at neat rows of drip hose attached to a header hose, which in turn is attached to the main tap hose.

The distance apart of each major planting row depends very much on the type of garden you already have or are planning to create. Essentially, multiply the number of major planting rows in the garden by the row length to get the total length of drip hoses you'll need.

Fortunately, you can buy kits with a filter and flow control and different lengths of hose. If you have a large area to cover, you might need more than one kit. Alternatively, you can buy the separate items — filter, hose, emitters and clamps — depending on how much you need. But stick to the same brand so all the parts are compatible. Virtually all brands of dripper pipe available have pressure-compensated emitters. So regardless of the pressure within the pipe, a consistent flow of water will be emitted. Depending on what brand you have, the quantity per dripper is usually between 2 and 3 L (4 and 5 pt) per hour.

Water will drip from the hose more uniformly when the rows are level or just slightly downhill. If your garden is on a slope, even if it's only a 1–2 per cent grade, consider running the hoses along the contour or around the slope, instead of up and down.

OPPOSITE Here's a couple of typical irrigation plans to give you an idea of how to design a system for your own garden.

handy hint

Before heading off to your local store, it's worthwhile ascertaining how much water your tap can deliver in a minute. Gather a container of known volume — say, a 10-L (4-gall) bucket — then time how long it takes to fill the container from the tap you're running the system from.

Spacing the emitters

I'll give you some specific guidelines for spacing the emitters for different plants, but there's one important rule of thumb that applies to all plants — they must be watered evenly. If you water a tree on only one side, the roots will flourish on that side. Eventually, the imbalance will make the tree unstable and unsafe, and it could fall over in a high wind because the roots haven't anchored it into the soil properly.

Bed cultures and flower plantings

If you're irrigating a garden bed, it's best to space drip hoses 20–30 cm (8–12 in) apart, with the emitters spaced 30 cm apart within each hose. It's more efficient if you position the hoses so that the emitters within each hose or line create a zigzag pattern. Always ensure that the emitters are placed within each plant's root zone.

Fruit and ornamental trees

Unlike garden beds, fruit and ornamental trees often require more emitters for their root zone. This is where additional plug in emitters come in handy. Instead of using more materials than you need by running out additional drip hoses, you can install as many emitters as the trees need.

The number you'll need depends entirely on the size of the tree: a small tree or shrub will need one emitter for every 76 cm (2½ ft) of canopy diameter, while larger ornamental and fruit trees with a canopy spread of 5 m (15 ft) or more will need six emitters. Just remember to calculate the quantity of water your tap or water source can provide each hour. There's no point in installing a system that needs 2000 L (440 gall) of water per hour when your tap can only provide 1000 L (220 gall). If this becomes the case with your system, then the only thing you can do is split the system into two areas and operate them one after another.

Once you start drip irrigating a tree, new feeder roots will become concentrated in the soil near the emitters so they can supply water to it. Try to start drip irrigation in early spring so the new roots can become established before summer, otherwise the tree could become stressed in hot weather.

To calculate the flow rate for your trees, multiply the number of emitters required by the rated output per emitter. This will give you the flow rate needed to irrigate all your trees and shrubs simultaneously. For example, if you have 12 trees for which 72 emitters are required, and each emitter has a rated output of 4.5 L (1 gall) per hour at 10.3 g per square cm or 103 kpa (15 lb per square inch), the flow rate will be 327 L (72 gall) per hour or 5 L (1.2 gall) per minute. You might like to grab a calculator for that one. In this case, a 13-mm (½-in) main line is perfectly sufficient.

An even easier option is to buy some pressure-compensated drip hosing. This stuff is usually brown and comes with the emitters already installed. Provided there's enough water flowing through the lines, they'll release a consistent quantity of water. These hoses are usually set at 2–4 L (4–7 pt) per hour, and the emitter spacings are usually 30 or 40 cm (8 or 12 in) apart. I suggest using the 30-cm spacing, as 40 cm can be too far apart. Even if the gap between plants is 1–1.5 m (4–5 ft), the roots will spread out from the stems in a wide radius, so you won't be wasting water.

Choosing emitters

Your best criteria for choosing the type of emitter to use are durability and ease of installation. Most emitters are either attached to the lateral, or connected in-line by cutting the pipe and connecting the emitter to the pipe. If you go for the latter, you could be looking at the extra cost of clamps to hold the emitters in place.

PREVIOUS SPREAD You can have a temperate-style garden in a hot climate — it's just a matter of selecting and grouping the appropriate plants.

OPPOSITE Roses perform well in a hot climate and suit a formal design, like this beautiful white and pink garden.

handy hint

Regardless of the system you have, the last thing you should do before plugging up the hose ends is to turn on the water. This will flush out any foreign particles that could otherwise block the hose.

If you haven't grouped your plants into zones according to their watering requirements — we cover this topic in 'Smart gardening', on pages 180–3 — you'll need to vary the number of emitters. Just install more emitters near plants requiring more water.

The soil factor

Your soil type is important too. If you have a clay soil, the water from the emitters will spread across the surface before being absorbed very deeply. This is due to capillary action. With sandy soil, on the other hand, gravity draws the water down through the larger spaces between the grains. So in a sandy soil, an emitter will water any area that's about 38 cm (15 in) in diameter, but in a clay soil it'll be more like 60 cm (2 ft).

If you haven't mulched your soil, it's best to bury the drip lines about 7–10 cm (3–4 in) deep. If you've done the right thing and mulched to a thickness of 8 cm (3 in), then bury the pipes a few centimetres into the soil beneath the mulch. If any lines have been damaged by spades or rodents, it's easy to replace them with a couple of connectors and a new section of tubing.

How much to water

You and I both know that nothing checks a plant's growth faster than lack of water. If we had the ability to store enough water to ensure an annual surplus, we would supply just enough water to maintain uniform soil moisture in the root zone — that is, each day we

Sea holly (*Eryngium planum*).

would replace the amount of moisture used by the plant the previous day. We would also be pruning like mad, as the growth rates would be phenomenal. But we need to find the happy medium, where the garden's water consumption reflects your district's rainfall. That is, at certain times of the year when there's plenty of rainfall, expect higher growth rates within your garden and store as much water as you can to supplement the garden during the dry parts of the year. Working out how much your garden needs, or how much different parts need, depends on many factors, such as:

- soil type and its rate of delivery;
- climate;
- season (plants need 3–4 times as much water in hot weather as in cold);
- weather conditions, such as rainfall, wind and humidity; and
- types and sizes of plants — vegetables will need a lot more irrigation than established shrubs and trees.

When to water

The ideal time to water is early morning, from 6 to 8 am: less water loss occurs due to evaporation and wind drift in the morning because it's cooler and less windy, and the leaves will dry quickly. Evening watering is also fairly efficient, but plants that are susceptible to leaf disease are more likely to be infected if their leaves stay wet for too long. The least efficient watering time is during the heat of the day when evaporation is rapid.

Extending the life of the system

The life of your drip system will be extended by:

- good design;
- proper filtering;
- being careful with gardening tools so you don't puncture the lines;
- mulching over the plastic lateral drip lines to shield them from sunlight and frost;
- regularly flushing lines; and
- draining lines if you experience freezing winters.

The owners of this rainwater tank excavated under their verandah so it would be out of sight. With a capacity of 17 000 L (4490 gall), it fills after only a few hours of heavy rain. The gauge at right indicates the water level.

Rainwater harvesting and storage systems

The appropriate rainwater tank system, when combined with an irrigation system, should see you through all but the worst drought, and holding rainwater in your own tanks has many advantages.

In most regions, enough rainwater can be captured to significantly reduce or eliminate the need for using town water in gardens. Furthermore, compared to grey water, distributing and applying rainwater is much more straightforward. There aren't so many plumbing regulations and restrictions because using rainwater benefits the groundwater supplies and reduces the quantity of stormwater pollution in the local waterways.

The only downside of using rainwater is having enough space to store the stuff. If you want to be serious about using rainwater then you need to hold at least 9000 L (1980 gall). On the other hand, any quantity of rainwater storage that helps to reduce demand on town water supplies is a plus. The ideal volume will depend on your type of garden and the local rainfall pattern. For instance, if you live in a tropical or Mediterranean climate, then you'll want to catch and store as much as possible to use during the dry period of the year. Remember that your goal is to be able to rely completely on rainfall to water your garden, so you should keep this rainwater for special occasions and for establishing plants (see page 186–7).

Once again, drip irrigation systems are best suited for most residential applications. They require less storage volume for the same area than sprinkler applicators. If your land has the right topography then you won't even need a pump to deliver the water. You can set up a simple, affordable system where you siphon the water from the tank via a hose or into water cans.

Collecting rainwater from the roof is the norm in most urban areas. Rather than taking a 'hit and giggle' approach, I strongly suggest you calculate how much water you could actually catch upon your roof and how much you need. A quick search on the internet will reveal lots of websites that'll help you to calculate this important information.

Buying, setting up and operating a rain tank system will probably cost you more than using town water for irrigation, at least to begin with, but if municipal water costs continue to rise and water utilities set up conservation fee structures and restrictions, it won't be long before your system starts paying for itself. Also, you might qualify for a rebate. Check with your local council or water utility.

Of course, installing a system is less expensive if it's part of the initial design and construction of a building. Usually retrofit systems are more expensive and may not complement the building or overall site design. Before installing one, don't forget to check with your local council to see if you need a building permit.

The best place to install your tank is near an existing downpipe and in the shade, as heat will encourage the growth of algae in the tank water while the sun's UV rays will degrade the tank itself. You should desludge the tank and catchment system (including the roof and gutters) every 2–3 years.

What you need

These are the sorts of fittings you might need for your rain tank system.

GUTTER MESH SYSTEMS help to keep gutters free of leaves and other debris.

RAIN HEADS prevent leaves and debris from entering gutter downipes.

INSECT PROOFING on all inlets and outlets prevents mosquitoes breeding.

A FIRST FLUSH DEVICE will divert the first 45 L (10 gall) of water, taking with it pollutants from the roof.

A TANK OVERFLOW PIPE will divert any overflow to the stormwater drains.

If you're using rainwater to flush toilets, then you may need a tank top-up system that augments the tank with mains water whenever the amount of water in the tank hits a designated minimum level.

Grey water

The jury is still out on whether grey water is the solution to keeping our gardens alive during these dry times. Me? I'm not too sure. But I'm giving it a go, and I admit I'm getting mixed results. I would much rather see the whole community collecting, treating and reusing waste waters rather than individual homes pumping waste water into our soils.

Let's have a look at what it's all about.

warning

Grey water must not be stored, as the bacteria and other micro-organisms reproduce very quickly. This results in a significant health hazard.

OPPOSITE Stonecrop (*Sedum spectabile* 'Autumn Joy').

What is grey water?

Grey water is simply the waste water that comes from the kitchen, laundry and bathroom sinks as well as the bath, shower, washing machine and dishwasher. Imagine what goes down the drain each time you take a shower — dirt and body oils, hair and lint, soap and detergent products, such as shampoo and conditioner. On top of that there are probably disinfectants and chemical cleaners like bleaches.

Normally all this waste water is removed from your home via the sewerage system, because it contains impurities and pathogens that are considered pollutants and at least potentially infectious.

Lots of people who recycle grey water have a fairly basic system in place: they might use the children's bath water on the garden, or run all the water from the washing machine's last rinse directly onto the lawn. But what they're not taking into account is that the grey water they're using might be contaminated waste that can also lead to soil degradation.

Laundry

Obviously, the water from the second rinse in your washing machine is going to be much better quality than the water from the washing cycle, which may contain higher concentrations of soap, sodium, phosphate, surfactants, ammonia and nitrogen as well as suspended solids, lint and oxygen-demanding bacteria. If you let this water onto your garden untreated, you're unleashing a public health risk as well as creating environmental havoc in your garden. Just remember that grey water contains both micro-organisms and the nutrients they feed on.

Swimming pool

The filtration backwash water from the average backyard swimming pool contains high concentrations of micro-organisms and chemicals such as pool chemicals, body

This formal cactus garden is designed around its water features — a circular pond and a terraced rill.

oils, hair and lint. Due to the quantity of water surge when backwashing a pool's filtration system and the laws pertaining to immediate dispersal of grey water, it's best to avoid this waste-water source.

Land application systems

Because the amount of grey water generated by each household varies so much, it's important to determine how much your household generates before a land application system is designed and installed. There are sites on the internet that will help.

Typically, though, you'll need an in-line filter to handle the solid particles in the grey water, and you'll need to check it frequently to keep it from getting blocked. Also biofilms created by micro-organisms may develop inside pipes and drippers and eventually clog the system.

Generally there are two types of delivery systems.

Gravity diversion device (GDD)

This system incorporates a hand-activated valve, switch or tap, which is fitted to the outlet of the waste pipe of, say, the laundry tub. You simply switch the device so that the water is diverted by gravity from the laundry tub to the diversion line and the dedicated land application system instead of the sewer.

Gravity diversion devices must not be installed below the 'S' bend on any plumbing fitting as this would allow sewer gases to enter your home — with potentially fatal consequences.

Pump diversion device

This device incorporates a surge tank to cope with sudden influxes of grey water, which are then distributed by a pump to a subsurface land application system. The surge tank must not operate as a storage tank. Kitchen water is not really suitable for collection in a pump diversion device because it will clog the device with fats, oils and food particles. Residues in the device cause foul odours and attract vermin. If you want to use this device with kitchen water, you must also install a domestic grey water treatment system or pass the waste water through a grease arrestor.

Regardless of the origin of the grey water, it must be screened as it enters a surge tank before it's distributed by pump to the subsurface land application system.

Pros and cons of grey water

Grey water is a potential garden-saving water but it comes at a cost.

- Filtering the crap from it is a chore, and if the various screens and filters are not cleaned often, the job becomes quite a foul affair.
- The cost of maintaining the system will add up over time.
- The residues within your soil — in particular, sodium — will also accumulate over time.

If you want to head down this path I suggest you avoid using kitchen water and washing-machine waste water as the lint is an absolute nightmare to filter out and the detergents in laundry powders will muck up your soil pH levels. Stick to using the shower and bath water. It's much easier to filter out and contains far fewer hazards.

Managing plants during drought

For those gardeners who are stuck in a drought with strict water restrictions and no water tank, here are some tips for keeping your garden alive.

1. Irrigate highly visible, drought-sensitive and intensively managed areas first. For instance, plants near house walls, footpaths and other reflective surfaces will dry out much faster than plants in the middle of a large lawn. Slopes, raised beds and hilly areas will also dry out much faster.
2. Give turf a lower priority. Although drought sensitive, turf is cheaper to replace than trees and shrubs.
3. Irrigate trees and shrubs after they start to wilt. If they're not watered, the leaves — starting with the oldest and most exposed leaves — will brown and eventually fall. This reduction in leaf cover helps the plant to conserve water but is also a sign of serious damage.
4. If your plants are well established in a well drained soil and were irrigated prior to the drought, a

thorough watering once every two weeks will usually keep them alive. If the soil is shallow or structurally poor, however, you need to water once every 1–2 weeks. But if there is reduced humidity and the daytime temperature is above 30°C (86°F) and the nightime temperature above 21°C (70°F), you'll need to water more frequently.

5 Get rid of groundcovers around trees and shrubs. Kill or remove any grass around them to reduce competition for water (creating a no-till situation) and put organic mulch 8 cm (3 in) deep around the base after watering, all the way to the drip line, if possible.

6 Do not prune plants in extremely hot, dry weather. If you do, and it rains, these plants may put on new growth that will not have a chance to harden off before late autumn.

7 On new construction sites, give special consideration to places where topsoil has been removed; soil has been added (often this is subsoil from someone else's excavation); soil has been compacted; construction materials have been buried; and any paving has been installed.

8 Avoid overwatering. Overwatering plants in poor soils is easy, and proper aeration is almost impossible. Poor soils often have wet spots, and the plant ends up dying from excess water, even during dry periods.

9 If you find the soil is repelling the water you're applying, then lightly loosen your soil before watering. For example, you can till, bore holes or hoe. The less tilling you do after loosening, the better. To help prevent compaction, avoid working with or walking on soils when they are wet.

10 If you watered your trees and shrubs shallowly during the first part of the dry season, you need to wean them gradually from this schedule. For example, if you watered plants twice a week during summer for one hour, cut back to once a week, then once every two weeks and finally, to once a month. Water only until no more water soaks into the soil. After that, water merely runs off, so it's time to move to a new spot.

11 Avoid using antitranspirants during very hot weather. Even though these materials are recommended for retarding the rate of transpiration, you could do more damage to your plants by creating a mini-greenhouse effect and heating them up drastically. Many of these products are waxy, coating leaves and stomata with an impermeable layer that reduces air and water exchange, thus reducing photosynthesis. On a 32–38°C (90–100°F) day, this waxy layer could raise the leaf temperature too high.

12 This may seem obvious to some, but I'll say it anyway: do not plant new trees and shrubs during summer.

PREVIOUS SPREAD Succulents can be grown in most climates, provided the soil is very well drained and there is ample sun and air movement.

OPPOSITE *Pennisetum advena* 'Rubrum'.

TOP RIGHT *Dahlia* 'Bishop of Llandaff'.

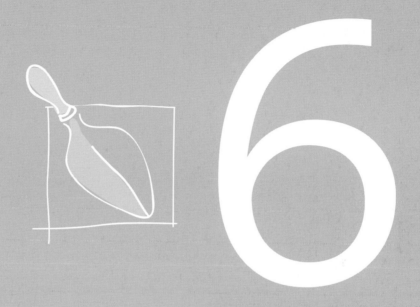

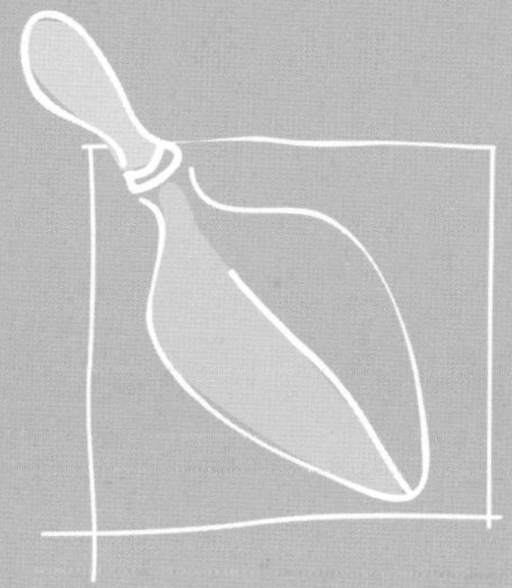

6

Smart gardening

Smart gardening

You can make your garden more water-efficient by planting appropriate species and employing good horticultural practices.

Have you ever wondered how much water you use in the garden, and how that compares with your total usage? Studies show that up to 50 per cent of town water consumed in homes is used outside. But before you swallow that lump forming in your throat, the water isn't totally dedicated to watering the garden: filling swimming pools and washing the car also consume their fair share of water.

The problem is that up until the last ten years or so, most of the garden plants we appreciate and cultivate were well suited to a cool temperate climate with regular rainfall, or a Mediterranean climate with moist winters and dry summers. That's all right if your garden enjoys a cool temperate or Mediterranean climate. But if you happen to garden in an area with cool winters and very humid summers, then you'll need to look that much harder to find plants that are both garden-worthy and water-efficient.

'Why can't I just plant natives?' I hear you ask. Of course you can and, yes, many of them are water-efficient and perform well in their natural habitat, but are they garden-worthy specimens? Will they stand the test of time? Will they grow too large? Will they prove to be a problem by maturing faster than other plants, making the garden look out of balance and proportion?

These days there are many beautiful and garden-worthy native plants available. Unfortunately, there are also just as many duds. If I haven't told you before, I may as well now: it's much cheaper and wiser to learn from other gardeners' mistakes by strolling around your neighbourhood, checking out which plants do well and which are best avoided. If you're not completely sure about the plant, simply hang around looking at it for a while. It won't be long before the owner wanders out to find out why you're casing the place. Once you've assured them it's the plant you're interested in and not the plasma TV in their living room, they'll tell you as much as they know about the plant. Why? Because people love it when someone else admires something in their possession.

We all need to rethink the way we approach garden design and planting. But it doesn't mean you have to transform your garden into a Tex-Mex landscape, with cacti and other low-water-use plants, mulched with pebbles. It's simply a matter of creating a garden or landscape that uses little supplemental water, and that's achieved by careful planning and sensible gardening practices, such as planting appropriate species and using compost and mulch. But more on that shortly.

Did you know?

Every year, an average home swimming pool loses its entire capacity to evaporation. If such a pool were covered, however, only half its capacity would be lost.

PREVIOUS SPREAD Dense plantings reduce evaporation and the drying effects of wind. They also require less mulch.

OPPOSITE You can grow a cottage garden with water-efficient plants, such as different varieties of salvia.

Xeriscaping

First, I'll tell you about xeriscaping, the original concept developed by Nancy Leavitt and Denver Water, an American public utility, in the 1980s. The term comes from the Greek word *xeris*, which means dry or arid, and the 'scape' in landscape. According to studies conducted in the 1990s, a xeriscaped garden can save between 25 and 42 per cent of total household water consumption, so more and more city councils and other groups concerned about water conservation are madly promoting xeriscaping as a technique.

As Denver Water own the term, I'll pay homage to the people who developed the design principle and replace 'xeriscaping' with 'smart gardening'.

The principles of smart gardening

We're not talking about a particular garden style here. Smart gardening is all about conserving water and external resources — whether you have a cottage garden, a low-maintenance courtyard, a tropical jungle or a sprawling suburban garden planted in a formal design. So you can have any style of garden you like; it will simply use much less water.

The seven principles used to develop smart gardening are good horticultural practices that can be applied to the environment and microclimate you live in.

1 Employ sound landscape planning and design.
2 Make soil improvements.
3 Reduce turf to appropriate areas.

Crocosmia, *Buddleja davidii*, *Aloe* sp., *Carex* sp. and *Phormium* sp. will thrive in a subtropical climate.

Purple coneflower (*Echinacea purpurea*).

4 Select plants appropriate for the climate, and group them according to their water needs.
5 Practise efficient irrigation.
6 Use mulches.
7 Carry out appropriate garden maintenance.

Before you embark on making your smart garden, you need to plan and design it.

1 Planning and design

Whether you're designing a garden or a house, the same rules apply. You need a plan. Just like a journey with a known destination, you still need a map to find your way to the goal. Even if you think you can keep a plan stored in your mind, you know you're fooling yourself — you've got to write it down. A carefully documented plan provides direction and guidance, and will ensure that you co-ordinate and implement water-conserving techniques in your garden. With this plan you can easily determine the schedule, the materials required and, of course, how much it's all going to cost.

You can't design your garden without a plan.

When I say carefully documented, I don't mean scaled to pinpoint accuracy with pretty colours. I mean a simple map of your garden. If you have a surveyor's plan of your property then you're halfway there. Simply lay some tracing paper over the survey and start tracing. Failing that, check with your local council in case they keep surveys in their archives. If you still have no joy, engage a surveyor to provide one. The cost will depend on the size of your property, the information required and the topography (that is, whether your site is steep or flat).

If you're keen to do it yourself, look at your property's conveyancing documents. You should find an A4-sized plan outlining the boundaries of your property and its aspect (where north is). The next step is to buy some graph and tracing paper. I reckon either ½- or 1-cm increments are the easiest to work with as you can also quickly calculate the surface areas by counting the squares — that is, 1 square = 1 square metre. (Or, if you don't use metric measures, use graph paper marked in inches so that 1 square = 1 square yard.)

Chances are your plan will need to be larger than A4. Either draw two plans — one for the front and one for the back — or change the scale from 1:100 to 1:200. On your scale diagram indicate north and mark the major elements of your landscape — for example, your house, shed, garage, driveway, footpaths, decks or patio and existing trees, anything you plan to keep in your garden.

There are other things worth plotting on the plan — tap locations, stormwater downpipes and sumps, services, fences, walls, slopes and, most importantly, anything outside your boundary that affects how your garden will perform, such as large trees, which create shade and have higher water requirements, and the size and aspect of your neighbours' buildings, which also create shade and cold and hot wind tunnels. Your neighbours might have a wretched air-conditioning unit blowing hot air off the Sahara Desert in summer, or they might be stickybeaks and you need some privacy. On the other hand, there could be some benefits, such as harvestable stormwater runoff.

For more detail on the design process, see page 171.

2 Soil

If you grew impatient and skipped the first chapter on soils, then you've just missed a ladder and landed on the snake's head. So back you go and learn about the most important topic in this book.

3 Turf

I've heard it time and time again. Some so-called garden experts on TV and radio say we should rid our gardens of wasteful turf. But I'm going defend the lawn's presence within the garden by providing some facts and realistic arguments. I don't mean the traditional look of grass, running all the way from the gutter to the front door. I mean an area of grass that's positioned to take advantage of the best possible growing conditions while at the same time accommodating your family's needs.

Here's an important fact to consider: your family needs enough lawn so your kids and pets can play and exercise and discover. (If your children need more space to kick a ball, then take them down to the football field or park. Who knows? You may just get to meet a neighbour.) When I say exercise, I mean simple stuff, like walking barefoot on healthy grass or wrestling with your kids. Gardens are for living, not show.

And here's another fact: turf also plays an important role in cooling the local environment, reducing erosion and preventing glare from the sun. Other groundcover plants can perform these functions but they can't provide a play area. So consider where you would like a turf area, how large it should be and how it will be used and in which seasons. You'll then be prepared to limit turf to useful spaces and be able to determine which grasses will best serve your needs.

The subdivided block we live on is 0.03 hectare (0.081 acre). I love it because there's enough gardening space to keep me busy but not enough to enslave me. My cottage garden is 12 x 9 m (39 x 29 ft), hosts over

If you have the space, include a lawn that's large enough for your kids to use as a mini playground.

90 different species of plants and still accommodates 18 square metres (21.5 square yards) of zoysia turf.

Now, earlier I mentioned the current trend of replacing lawn with paving, pebbles, scree or mulch. Had I taken this advice, we'd probably require an air-conditioner, which would pollute the atmosphere with a few extra tonnes of carbon dioxide annually, and we would have increased our wasteful stormwater runoff. And I wouldn't be able to indulge in one of the best experiences you can enjoy in your own garden — tea on the lawn before noon and Pimms before sunset. Finally, let's also remember that every plant plays its role in helping to absorb society's belches of carbon dioxide.

If there were a groundcover plant that required less water than grass to prosper and still survive the trauma of two young boys playing on it, I would be cultivating that instead. Our patch of zoysia receives next to no irrigation and provides our family with a quality of life that paving pebbles or mulch couldn't achieve. I can assure you there's a lawn variety that best suits your needs and water availability — just do some research.

TOP Among the plants in my perennial border are Westonbirt or red-stemmed dogwood (*Cornus alba* 'Sibirica'), Callery pear (*Pyrus calleryana*) 'Chanticleer' and Sarabande maiden grass (*Miscanthus sinensis* 'Sarabande'), an old favourite, French lavender (*Lavandula dentata*), and a handful of other treasures in an area that's 5 x 2 m (5.5 x 2 yd).

BOTTOM Terracing saves water and increases the soil volume.

Statice, amaranthus and *Strobilanthes gossypinus* are among the wide variety of species in this bed.

4 Plants

Another principle of smart gardening is to group plants according to their water requirements — in other words, you need to group them into hydrozones. For example, azaleas, camellias and gardenias prefer a consistently moist soil (note I didn't say wet or damp). Make friends with a horticulturalist at your local nursery or garden centre and they'll help you with what grows best in your district.

A good tip is to place low-water-using plants together in areas that tend to be constantly dry, such as adjacent to walls and fences, or that are hardest to access with irrigation or hand-watering. Also, place high-water-using plants in a low-lying area where natural drainage will help keep the soil moist.

Reduce the likelihood of overwatering by thoroughly thinking through and investigating your plants' needs before you start. I must stress this point: water-efficient plants still require plenty of water for 12–16 weeks after planting. This is called the 'establishment period' and is of paramount importance (see page 186–7).

5 Irrigation

I cover this in more detail in the irrigation chapter (see pages 130–59), but here are the salient points. If you're installing an automatic sprinkler system, plan for this at the design stage if you can. Use appropriate irrigation methods and divide your garden into zones for turf and high- and low-water-use plants. For example, low-pressure sprinklers that irrigate the turf close to the ground are best for grass, while drip, micro-spray and bubbler emitters are appropriate for watering trees and shrubs. If you're watering by hand, use the setting that gives you big drops, as fine spray evaporates more easily.

Train your garden to cope with less water by watering for a longer time each session but as infrequently as possible. This will allow the water to soak deeper into the soil, encouraging the roots to give chase. Always try to water between 9 pm and 9 am, especially in summer, as you'll lose a lot less water to evaporation. If you have an automatic irrigation system, install a shut-off device that's activated by rain, and remember to program it to suit the changing seasons.

6 Mulches

Been there, done that — see pages 70–4. Mulching is essential for smart gardening. It helps to keep plant roots cool, prevents soil from crusting, minimises the amount of evaporation and reduces weed growth. Mulch also gives beds a finished look and improves the visual appeal of your garden. The final depth of your mulch should be 8 cm (3 in).

7 Maintenance

For the first couple of years, your smart garden will require all the usual maintenance — weeding, irrigation, pruning, fertilising and pest control. Once your plants start to mature, sending their roots deep into the soil, they'll need less water and there'll be less room for weeds to spring up.

Converting to smart gardening

It's worth noting that your garden will not convert itself; it will adapt to the new set of conditions. It's you, the gardener, who needs converting. Your garden will come along for the ride.

Adapting your garden to a smart one takes time, planning and money. You might want to start from scratch and hire a horticulturalist or landscape designer, or you may prefer to work on one area at a time yourself. Either way, the aim is to end up with a beautiful garden that uses less water and requires less maintenance.

Here's a three-year plan.

Year 1: Planning the garden

This is the big one — the year you draw up the plan of your smart garden and start to implement it. There are four main tasks ahead of you.

1. Design your new garden, or redesign areas in the existing garden.
2. Modify your existing irrigation system, or design a new one.
3. Decide which areas of high-water-use turf you need to remove.
4. Start creating new areas.

The design process

Your first task is to decide on the type of garden style you want. Look at books and magazines for inspiration, and keep a scrapbook of the plants and designs that appeal to you. If you're going to employ a professional landscaper to design your garden, then your ideas will help them to establish the look you're after, whether it's an informal native garden or a grand landscape in the English style.

Kangaroo paw (*Anigozanthos* sp.), *Salvia* 'Coral Nymph' and *Heliotrope arborescens*.

As a rule, autumn is the best time to prepare and plant, as the heat stresses of summer are behind you and the soil is still warm, which means party time for the soil organisms as well as vigorous root growth. If you're not too sure, talk to your local nursery or landscape professional about what time of year is best for removing turf and setting new plants, and how much water your chosen plants need in the first two years to become established.

Microclimate

If you plan to do all the work yourself, take the time to do some research — will your favourite trees and shrubs grow well in your microclimate? For instance, if you live in a cool temperate climate, you can't plant a tree that normally thrives in a tropical environment. So make a list of the features of your microclimate, such as:

- temperature;
- hours of sunlight;
- rainfall;
- prevailing winds;
- humidity; and
- frost and snow.

Note that different parts of your garden may have different climatic characteristics. For instance, in the southern hemisphere, the northern side receives more sun, so it probably has a warmer microclimate than the cooler southern side. Also in the southern hemisphere, the western side typically gets lots of hot afternoon sun and is well suited to arid landscaping. Eastern sides offer better environments for higher-water-use zones. And if you live in the northern hemisphere, it's the south side that cops the sun.

Site analysis

Next, analyse your site. Some factors to consider include:

ORIENTATION Does your garden face north or south? Depending on which hemisphere you live in, this will affect the amount of sun and shade in your garden.

TOPOGRAPHY Indicate on your site plan the high and low areas so you can work out drainage patterns as well as wet and dry spots.

ABOVE *Lomandra* 'Matt Rush'.

OPPOSITE These plants — gymea lilies, scaevola and *Poa* sp. — thrive on shallow soil and are watered by turf runoff.

SOIL Establish the soil type and structure in different parts of your garden. (For more information on soil, see 'All about soil'.)

VIEWS These include views of the garden from inside the house as well as views of neighbouring landscapes. For example, your neighbour might have a beautiful mature tree that you want to incorporate in your landscape.

At this point you have two choices: you can plan an entirely new landscape or you can develop greater water efficiency in the existing landscape. If it's a big garden or a project currently underway, incorporate both approaches. You can remodel the areas that have already been completed and adjust your plans for the next stages.

Garden 'rooms'

The next step is to think about how you'll use your garden. Do you want to include an outdoor eating area, or a play area for the children? Where should you put the clothesline and garbage bins?

This lawn is adjacent to bushland reserve so the mature eucalypts become part of the garden's landscape.

Make a list of your needs, taking into account the particular areas or garden 'rooms' you'd like to include:

- utility areas — clothesline, garbage and compost bins, storage;
- outdoor living areas — paved areas, pergolas, barbecue, seating;
- play areas — a grassy area where the kids can play safely, an interesting shrubbery that includes 'secret' spaces, a cubby house or play equipment; and
- any special features — a swimming pool or pond, or a vegetable patch or flower garden.

Another factor to consider at this stage is the position of paths, what landscape architects call 'desire lines'. People will always find the shortest, most convenient route from one part of the garden to another, especially if they're carrying a basket full of wet laundry, so there's no point in laying a meandering path from the laundry door to the clothesline. You'll just end up wearing a straight track across your lawn.

Other factors

If your garden has developed over time with little bits all over the place, you can simply change it around. But keep the following factors in mind while you're still in the planning stages.

PAVING AND MULCHES Don't plant areas unless it's necessary for functional or aesthetic reasons. Instead, use paving and mulches. On the other hand, don't use so much unshaded paving that your garden becomes hot and glary. Use plants to frame and shade paved areas, planting them densely to maximise the use of water.

SHELTER Provide shelter and shade in the form of pergolas, screens, climbing plants and windbreaks.

TRANSPLANTING You can easily transplant high-water-use plants in winter, as their root systems are shallow, but don't transplant hardy, drought-tolerant species because their root systems usually grow very deep. For example, most Australian native plants don't tolerate transplanting. Compare the time and effort required to prepare, dig and lift the species as well as the time required for the plant to recover from the shock of relocation, then the time to re-establish itself. Quite often it's better to spend the money on an advanced specimen and euthanise the other.

TURF Keep turf areas to a minimum and don't plant lawn in awkward little corners that will be hard to maintain. If you choose to convert some areas of lawn to a lower-water-use treatment, make sure that the replacement plants or ground treatments are more water-efficient than grass. Check this out with a member of your local nursery industry association.

Soil improvement

I covered this earlier, but just to remind you how important the soil is, I'll say it again. The better and deeper the soil preparation and improvement, the greater will be the plant's ability to perform and flourish. Plants in shallow or rocky soils, or in soils that have a compacted layer where roots cannot penetrate, will have poorer low-moisture endurance than those in deep, loose soils where roots can penetrate deeply and easily.

Since many landscapes have poor and shallow soils, soil improvement becomes important when you're establishing a low-water-use area. Dig or till the soil as deeply as possible before planting. If there's a compacted layer, break it up. If you're planting trees, dig holes as wide as possible, but no deeper than the tree's root ball.

Here's an example of a well established moderate-water-use garden in a cool climate.

In clay soils, don't dig holes with smooth sides, since the roots will circle the hole and fail to spread fully into the surrounding soil. Potted or field-grown trees or shrubs produced in very light or organic soils should be backfilled with a blend of 25 per cent potting mix to 75 per cent local improved soil around the root ball to aid establishment and stimulate thorough root expansion. These types of soil mixes are often called 'transitional soil blends'.

During the soil improvement process, test the soil to determine the existing pH and fertility levels. Then adjust the soils so they're most suitable for the plants you're adding to the landscape. You may have to adjust the pH and improve the soil fertility to ensure that establishing plants will survive moisture stress. (For more information, see page 25.)

An irrigation system

Unless you're a keen and capable do-it-yourself type, it's probably a good idea to get some professional advice on a watering system that's tailored to meet your garden's needs.

If you already have a system installed, you may be able to adapt it without completely replacing it. For example, you can adapt garden bed spray-heads to dripper systems with multiple outlet adapters and spaghetti tubes. It all depends on the size of your garden, how many different areas or watering zones you have (see 'Hydrozones' below), and how many you need to convert to smart gardening practices.

Hydrozones and plant selection

Basically, your water-efficient garden should be zoned according to three major water-use areas. Whether you're planning a new garden or adding new plants to an existing one, try to choose plants that can survive short periods of heat and drought.

A good choice for a low-water-use garden, clivias perform well in shallow, rocky soils.

Low-water-use plants

Only water the plants in this zone during the establishment period. After that, you'll have to rely on natural rainfall, even during drought. Plants to use in this zone are *Xylosma* sp., *Protea* sp., *Banksia* sp., *Grevillea* sp., *Metrosideros* sp., *Yucca* sp., *Agave* sp., lavender, geraniums (*Pelargonium* sp.), rosemary (*Rosmarinus* sp.), oleander (*Nerium* sp.) and *Clivia* sp.

The simplest way to determine which plants can survive in the garden without extra water is to observe native plants, existing mature gardens in your local area and roadside plantings. Please note that I said 'observe plants', not 'take plants'. It's a sad state of affairs when even plants are considered worth stealing from public reserves, council plantings and, worst of all, private gardens.

RIGHT These grasses are low-water-use plants.

BELOW Leylands, heliotrope, salvia, penstemon and *Strobilanthes anisophyllus* are all high-water-use plants.

Signs of wilting in turf

Once about a third of your turf starts to wilt, it's time to water. Here are the signs to look for.

- After someone walks across the grass, their footprints are still visible some time later.
- The lawn goes a bluish grey colour.
- The majority of leaf blades fold in half lengthways.

Moderate-water-use plants

Treat the plants in this zone as you would the ones in the low-water-use zone, but give plants requiring special care extra water. Most plants with large, deep root systems can cope with only being watered during heatwaves or extended dry periods. Some suggestions are *Hydrangea* sp. (once established), *Murraya* sp., box (*Buxus* sp.), roses (*Rosa* sp.), *Camellia* sp., *Viburnum* sp., *Rondeletia* sp., New Zealand flax (*Phormium* sp.), evergreen magnolias (such as *Magnolia grandiflora*), Chinese star jasmine (*Trachelospermum jasminoides*), most perennial salvias (*Salvia* sp.), *Hibiscus* sp., *Plumbago* sp., ornamental grasses and *Agapanthus* sp.

High-water-use plants

Water these plants whenever they need it, but restrict them to highly visible areas around your home where you'll appreciate their colour and form, perhaps at the front entrance or around the outdoor entertaining area. Just about any plant that can survive cool temperate to subtropical climates is suitable for this zone — for example, deciduous magnolias (such as *Magnolia stellata*), *Gardenia* sp., *Dahlia* sp., culinary herbs like thyme and parsley, vegetables, showy annuals, ferns and *Rhododendron* sp.

Hydrozones in established gardens

If your garden is already established, you can still create water-use zones. For example, when plants die during drought periods, you can replace them with low-water-use plants. Or you can individually water precious specimens with high water needs. As I keep saying, you can make any garden more water efficient by improving

PREVIOUS SPREAD The moderate-water-use plants in this garden include gaura, tree germander, salvia and dusty miller.

LEFT Plant ferns in shaded, compost-rich soils where they can exploit runoff.

OPPOSITE This cottage garden is surviving very well on just rainfall, but at the end of summer the grass is starting to fade a little.

the soil, using mulches, reducing exposure to wind and blazing sun by providing shade and wind breaks, reassessing your watering practices and, if you're cashed up and have little spare time, installing an efficient irrigation system.

Turf selection and maintenance

Just like ornamental plants, turf can be zoned according to its water needs. However, regardless of the zone, you'll still need to irrigate the turf during the establishment period (and woe betide you if you've been cheap or lazy about soil preparation). After a couple of years, your turf will be mature enough to survive without any irrigation.

Low-water-use zone

If your turf is left to rely on natural rainfall, and you hit a drought period, here's what to expect.

- The turf will turn brown, especially if it doesn't receive water for two weeks or more.
- If the drought period is prolonged, the turf will change to a straw colour, signalling summer dormancy. Even though the grass blades are dead, sufficient rainfall should help the turf to recover.

Water-saving tips for lawns

- Mow less frequently and keep the cutting blades on the mower high, so that the turf stays tall. Mowing stresses the grass by increasing respiration and reducing root growth. Tall grass has deeper roots and shades the soil; short grass both dries out fast and heats up quickly.
- Keep the blades on your mower sharp. A clean cut heals faster and loses less water than a cut made by a dull blade.
- Fertilise turf with a complete lawn fertiliser in early to mid-spring and again in early autumn. Gardeners of the male gender should read the instructions and stick to what's recommended! 'More is better' is not a motto that applies to lawn food. Warm-season grasses such as couch, buffalo, kikuyu and zoysia benefit by receiving a tad more in spring and a little less in autumn, while the cool-season grasses such as fescues and ryes prefer the opposite. Regardless of what type of lawn you have or what brand of fertiliser you use, always —always — ensure the turf gets a decent watering immediately after you apply the fertiliser. I usually race out and feed lawns when the rain's about to fall. This saves time and water, and washes the granules off the grass foliage and into the root zone.

If you're unsure about which fertiliser to use, ask the nursery horticulturalist (not the hardware bloke or the casual weekend staff) which brand is appropriate.

Choose a grass that's suitable for your climate.

- The growth rate will slow down, so it's important to mow less often. Mowing dormant grass may damage the turf.
- In extreme conditions, the ground may crack, drying out the soil and resulting in loss of turf cover.

Some suitable species for this zone are zoysia and some couch varieties.

Medium-water-use zone

How much you water the turf in this zone depends on the amount of rainfall. The idea is to train the turf to cope with about four deep waterings over summer. That's about 15 cm (6 in) of water. If the grass wilts, then folds or rolls, apply about 35 mm (1½ in) of water in order to wet the soil to a depth of about 30 cm (1 ft). If the water just runs off, apply 13 mm (½ in) of water every day for three days running.

Suitable species are those used in a low-water-use zone, such as zoysia grass and some couch species, as well as kikuyu, varieties of buffalo grass, some cultivars of tall fescue and Kentucky blue grass.

High-water-use zone

Water turf in this zone at the first sign of wilting. If there's no rainfall, apply about 25 mm (1 in) of water a week.

Use tall fescue, hard fescue, Kentucky blue grass, perennial ryegrass, zoysia, couch, bent grass and soft-leaf buffalo.

Mulching

Mulching turf? Most modern mowers have a mulching setting, whereby the lawn clippings are directed back down into the lawn. This increases the amount of organic matter and reduces evaporation.

You can find out more about mulch on pages 70–4.

On a hot day, a water feature in the deep shade of a large old tree, underplanted with shade-loving plants, is a cool, peaceful retreat.

How will I know when my plants are established?

Check out the new shoots on transplanted plants during the first flush of new growth in spring. As plants become established, the length of new growth will increase. Once this happens, you should be able to cut down on watering.

Irrigation

As I've said before, water during the cooler parts of the day — preferably between 9 pm and 9 am, when less moisture is lost to evaporation. As a general guideline, in dry weather your garden needs about 25 mm (1 in) of water per week. In very hot weather, you can increase this to 5 cm (2 in) a week.

Make sure your plants are getting the right amount of water. You can check exactly how much by either measuring the amount of water that falls into cans or jars or by digging out a small amount of soil with a trowel (see page 136).

Shade

Remember, your goal with smart gardening is to reduce moisture loss. Another way to achieve this is to design your garden with shade, which can be provided by plants such as trees, shrubs and climbers or by built structures, such as pergolas, arbours and screens. But plants are cooler. You can test this out by going for a walk in a park on a really hot day. The air under trees will be cooler, not just because of the shade they provide but also because they release moisture as they transpire, cooling both the atmosphere and the soil. This has the added benefit of reducing the amount of evaporation from plants in their shade.

You can also use shade to cool down hard surfaces, such as paved areas, which in summer can radiate heat for hours after the sun goes down.

Hard surfaces and heat barriers

There are other ways to reduce heat build-up around hard surfaces in your garden.

- Choose light-coloured paving as it absorbs less heat and cuts down on glare.
- Make paths with organic materials, such as bark mulch, composted sawdust and wood chips.
- Create heat barriers between hard surfaces and vulnerable plants by planting hardy hedges or covering low fences with heat-tolerant climbers. For instance, separate a driveway from a lawn with a hedge of *Murraya* sp.

Maintenance

These maintenance tips will also help you to save water in the garden.

- Healthy plants tolerate drought better than diseased or damaged ones, so keep a look out for pests and diseases, and don't run the mower or the string trimmer up against the trunks of trees.
- Although pruning helps to reduce the amount of moisture lost from foliage, proceed carefully: if you get carried away with the secateurs, you could leave the plant open to more sunlight and moisture loss.
- Don't fertilise during periods of drought. Wait for the cooler weather of autumn and spring, and make sure there is enough moisture in the soil for it to absorb the nutrients you're adding. When you do fertilise, use a low-nitrogen and, preferably, organic-based product: fertilising promotes plant growth and then, logically, increases the plants' need for water. Synthetic fertilisers are basically a collection of various salts. Apply too much and the fertiliser will actually draw water from the plants' roots. This terrible situation is known as exosmosis.

OPPOSITE Self-seeding sweet Alice (*Lobularia maritima*) softens the edge of this green and white garden bed. Other plants include a climbing China rose and euphorbia.

Year 2: Plant establishment

In the second year you'll be helping your new plants to establish themselves. You may also be adding new areas or converting old ones. If you planted trees and shrubs in the first year, start filling in beds with perennials.

The whole idea with plant establishment is to encourage your plants to send their roots deep into the soil. If you 'spoil' them with frequent, shallow watering, their roots will stay near the surface. Then along comes a really hot day or two, just when you happen to be away for the weekend, and bingo — the vulnerable plants will get badly scorched, their leaves turning yellow or brown along the margins. If you don't water immediately, they'll probably die. If the leaves have turned completely brown, it's probably too late.

So remember what I told you about hydrozones before, and water your plants accordingly.

What to do in a drought

If there's a drought on and you're living in an area with severe water restrictions, take these steps.

- Only water plants once they start to wilt.
- Let turf go dormant and concentrate your water allowance on saving your trees and shrubs. The turf will probably recover once it receives some decent rain, but if it doesn't, it'll be much cheaper to replace than trees and shrubs.
- Remove weak plants.
- Prune plants to reduce leaf area.

This path has been made from composted softwood sawdust (plantation grown, of course), which makes a nice spongy surface underfoot.

If you don't maintain your garden, nature will soon reclaim it

Maintenance

There are lots of maintenance jobs to take care of in the second year, but you can always reward yourself with a refreshing Pimms at the end of a productive day in the garden.

- Add more mulch.
- Weed beds regularly and remove any competitive plants that are causing problems.
- Review your irrigation schedule with an eye to cutting back on watering. Keep hand-watering any new or special plants, taking your cues from the plants themselves.
- Repair any leaks in your irrigation system.

Year 3: Plants fully established

This is the year your plants become fully established. Otherwise, it's much the same as the second year — continue with all your maintenance tasks, consult your master plan and start work on the next part of your garden. It's really not that tricky once you get your head around it.

And don't forget the 'professional help' option. It keeps families like mine fed.

7

Planting guide

Planting guide

Earlier on we learnt that the best and most economical way to select plants is to learn from the mistakes and victories of your neighbours' gardens and to check out what's available in your local garden centre or nursery. Use the phrase 'right plant, right place' as a mantra and it'll hold you in good stead. If the old mate down the road is growing ripper hydrangeas on the south-eastern side of his house with minimal supplementary watering, then that south-eastern spot is probably a winning spot for hydrangeas in your garden too.

Remember these important points.

1. When you spot a 'good doer' on a walk around the neighbourhood, make sure the spot in your garden matches the aspect and microclimate of the plant you've admired.
2. When they're young and establishing, most plants need plenty of water to ensure a deep and robust root system. Once they're established to maturity, and provided you have sufficient soil depths and no compaction problems, you should only have to water them during periods of extended drought or heatwave conditions. Even during these times, you may find that they can still cope without a drink.
3. Many plants have been labelled and generalised as water guzzlers by textbook or armchair commentators. Hydrangeas are a fine example. If you live near the coast and have deep sandy soils, you'll find that if you obey the rules of the establishment period, in three years or so your hydrangeas won't need watering. If you live on a soil that's compacted or quite shallow, however, they will need supplemental water all their lives.

Conversely, we're often told that succulents need very little water to survive. This may be true, but remember there's a big difference between a plant surviving and a plant growing. The more water you provide a succulent, the more it will consume. Aloes and agaves are great examples of this behaviour. Although they will tolerate drought and poor soil, they much prefer a regular drink and fertile soils.

In this section I've knocked up lists of appropriate plants for the four climate types that 98 per cent of us live in. Most of these treasures have a preference for a particular soil type. By now you should know that this soil type is a well drained loamy soil. You should also be sure that the soil in your garden is advancing towards that status. Remember the golden rule? Continual soil improvement will bring you greater water efficiencies. Complaining about your sandy or heavy clay soil without taking action to amend it means that you're not fair dinkum about your garden.

A word on annuals

Now, before you zip down to the nursery to buy a few punnets of some species I've suggested, determine where you're going to grow them, then get busy tickling the soil so you have a lovely seed bed prepared.

Why a seed bed? First, many of the varieties I've recommended won't be available in punnet form as they're either not that popular or are lousy for transplanting. If you want your annuals to be water-efficient and to flower well, you will need to sow them directly into the desired position, then thin the seedlings once they've germinated. How? Fear not, my champion gardener! The directions for sowing are clearly outlined on the seed packets. It's easy and extremely rewarding, believe me.

Most if not all of the annuals I've listed here have robust taproots that burrow deep into the soil in search of the precious wet stuff. If the plant is grown in a punnet or a pot first, the root system is retarded when it hits the edge of the pot and never develops properly.

Plants for a Mediterranean climate

Plants that have adapted to long, dry, hot summers and mild, moist winters are suitable for a Mediterranean-type climate.

Trees

Ash (*Fraxinus* sp.)
Atlas cedar (*Cedrus atlantica*)
Bay tree (*Laurus nobilis*)
Boab tree (*Brachychiton rupestris*)
Bottlebrush (*Callistemon* sp.)
Californian tree poppy (*Fremontodendron californicum*)
Canary Island date palm (*Phoenix canariensis*)
Cedar of Lebanon (*Cedrus libani*)
Chaste tree (*Vitex agnus-castus*)
Coastal banksia (*Banksia integrifolia*)
Crepe myrtle (*Lagerstroemia indica*)
Fig (*Ficus carica*)
Golden rain tree (*Koelreuteria paniculata*)
Gum tree (*Eucalyptus* sp.)
Holm oak (*Quercus ilex*)
Indian bean tree (*Catalpa bignonioides*)
Judas tree (*Cercis siliquastrum*)
Monkey puzzle tree (*Araucaria araucana*)
New Zealand cabbage tree (*Cordyline australis*)
Norfolk Island pine (*Araucaria heterophylla*)
Olive (*Olea* sp.)
Pencil pine (*Cupressus sempervirens*)
Strawberry tree (*Arbutus* sp.)
Wattles (*Acacia* sp.)

Shrubs

Banksia sp.
Beauty bush (*Kolkwitzia amabilis*)
Boronia sp.
Butterfly bush (*Buddleja davidii*)
California lilac (*Ceanothus* sp.)
Coastal rosemary (*Westringia* sp.)
Giant yucca (*Yucca elephantipes*)

CLOCKWISE FROM TOP *Hibiscus rosa-sinensis, Banksia integrifolia, Arbutus unedo* and *Cedrus atlantica.*

Grevillea sp., Western Australian varieties
Hawaiian hibiscus (*Hibiscus rosa-sinensis*)
Lavender (*Lavandula* sp.)
Leonotis sp.
Leucadendron sp.
Oleander (*Nerium oleander*)
Protea sp.
Rock rose (*Cistus* sp.)
Rosemary (*Rosmarinus* sp.)
Roses (*Rosa* sp.)
Spurge (*Euphorbia wulfenii*)
Syrian hibiscus (*Hibiscus syriacus*)
Tea tree (*Leptospermum* sp.)

Perennials and grasses

Beard tongue (*Penstemon* sp.)
Blue marguerite (*Felicia amelloides*)
Blue fescue (*Festuca glauca*)
Catmint (*Nepeta* sp.)
Coneflower (*Rudbeckia* sp.)
Cranesbill (*Geranium* sp.)
Feather grass (*Miscanthus sinensis*)
Feather reed grass (*Calamagrostis* x *acutiflora*)
Flax (*Linum perenne*)
Fountain grass (*Pennisetum alopecuroides*)
Geranium (*Pelargonium* sp.)
Globe artichoke (*Cynara cardunculus*)
Jerusalem sage (*Phlomis fruticosa*)
Kangaroo paw (*Anigozanthos* cultivars)
New Zealand flax (*Phormium tenax*)
Ornamental sages (*Salvia* sp.)
Oyster plant (*Acanthus mollis*)
Pincushion flower (*Scabiosa* sp.)
Purple coneflower (*Echinacea purpurea*)
Sea holly (*Eryngium giganteum*)
Tall bearded iris (*Iris germanica*)
Mullein (*Verbascum* sp.)
Wallflower (*Erysimum* sp.)
Wormwood (*Artemesia* sp.)
Yarrow (*Achillea millefolium*)

Annuals

Adonis sp.
Bachelor's buttons (*Gomphrena globosa*)
California poppy (*Eschscholzia californica*)
Cosmos (*Cosmos bipinnatus*)
Flanders or field poppy (*Papaver rhoeas*)
Love-in-a-mist (*Nigella damascena*)
Night-scented tobacco (*Nicotiana sylvestris*)
Opium poppy (*Papaver somniferum*)
Pigface (*Portulaca grandiflora*)
Pyrethrum daisy (*Chrysanthemum cinerariaefolium*)
Queen Annes lace (*Ammi majus*)
Spider flower (*Cleome hassleriana*)
Verbena (*Verbena* x *hybrida*)
Virginia stock (*Matthiola maritima*)

Groundcovers

Blanket flower (*Gaillardia* sp.)
Garden pinks (*Dianthus* sp.)
Golden marguerite (*Anthemis tinctoria*)
Ivy-leafed geranium (*Pelargonium peltatum*)
Morrocan glory vine (*Convolvulus sabatius*)
Oregano (*Origanum* sp.)
Seaside daisy (*Erigeron karvinskianus*)
Snow-in-summer (*Cerastium tomentosum*)
Soapwort (*Saponaria* sp.)
Treasure flower (*Gazania* sp.)

Climbers

Bougainvillea glabra
Cape honeysuckle (*Tecomaria capensis*)
Creeping fig (*Ficus pumila*)
Lady Banks rose (*Rosa banksiae*)
Trumpet flower (*Bignonia* sp.)
Wax vine (*Senecio macroglossus*)

OPPOSITE, CLOCKWISE FROM TOP LEFT *Cistus* sp., *Euphorbia wulfenii*, *Leptospermum scoparium*, *Penstemon* sp., *Rudbeckia* 'Rustic Dwarf' and *Westringea fruticosa*.

THIS PAGE, CLOCKWISE FROM TOP LEFT *Eschscholzia californica*, *Papaver somniferum*, *Anthemis tinctoria*, *Convolvulus* sp., *Nigella damascena*, *Dianthus* sp., *Ficus pumila* and *Cleome* sp.

Plants for coastal climates

Coastal climates generally involve both mild summers and winters, with a reasonably consistent rainfall throughout the year. But the down sides can be high humidity and windy conditions, often with salt-laden winds.

Trees

Bribie Island pine (*Callitris columellaris*)
Broad-leafed paperbark (*Melaleuca quinquenervia*)
Bunya pine (*Araucaria bidwillii*)
Coastal banksia (*Banksia integrifolia*)
Cottonwood (*Hibiscus tiliaceus*)
Lancewood (*Pseudopanax crassifolius*)
New Zealand cabbage tree (*Cordyline australis*)
Norfolk Island hibiscus (*Lagunaria patersonia*)
Norfolk Island pine (*Araucaria heterophylla*)
Swamp oak (*Casuarina glauca*)
Swamp paperbark (*Melaleuca ericifolia*)
Sydney golden wattle (*Acacia longifolia*)

Shrubs

Blue plumbago (*Plumbago auriculata*)
Coast tea tree (*Leptospermum laevigatum*)
Coastal rosemary (*Westringia* sp.)
Dragon tree (*Dracaena draco*)
Euryops sp.
Grevillea sp.
Hawaiian hibiscus (*Hibiscus rosa-sinensis*)
Heath banksia (*Banksia ericifolia*)
Honeysuckle banksia (*Banksia spinulosa*)
Indian hawthorn (*Raphiolepis indica*)
Marguerite daisy (*Argyranthemum* sp.)
Metrosideros sp.
Mock orange (*Murraya paniculata*)
Oleander (*Nerium oleander*)
Paperbark (*Melaleuca* sp.)
Ponytail palm (*Beaucarnea recurvata*)

THIS PAGE, CLOCKWISE FROM TOP *Lagunaria patersonia, Raphiolepis indica, Banksia spinulosa, Dianella* sp., *Agapanthus* sp. and *Metrosideros excelsia*.

OPPOSITE, CLOCKWISE FROM TOP LEFT *Indigofera* sp., *Crinum pedunculatum, Lobularia maritima, Scaevola aemula* and *Hardenbergia violacea*.

Protea sp.
Scarlet bottlebrush (*Callistemon citrinus*)
Vitex trifolia
Weeping bottlebrush (*Callistemon viminalis*)
Yucca sp.

Perennials and grasses

African lily (*Agapanthus* sp.)
Arthropodium sp.
Bird of paradise (*Strelitzia reginae*)
Cape daisy (*Osteospermum* sp.)
Flax lily (*Dianella* sp.)
Geranium (*Pelargonium* sp.)
Indigofera sp.
Lomandra longifolia 'Tanika'
New Zealand flax (*Phormium tenax*)
Stonecrop (*Sedum spectabile*)
Spurge (*Euphorbia wulfenii*)
Swamp lily (*Crinum pedunculatum*)

Annuals

Bachelor's buttons (*Gomphrena globosa*)
California poppy (*Eschscholzia californica*)
Cosmos (*Cosmos bipinnatus*)
Love-in-a-mist (*Nigella damascena*)
Pigface (*Portulaca grandiflora*))
Sweet Alice (*Lobularia maritima*)
Virginia stock (*Matthiola maritima*)

Groundcovers

African daisy (*Arctotis* sp.)
Blue eyes (*Evolvulus pilosus*)
Brachycome multifida
Fairy fan flower (*Scaevola aemula*)
Guinea gold vine (*Hibbertia scandens*)
Happy wanderer (*Hardenbergia violacea*)
Kangaroo lobelia (*Dampiera diversifolia*)
Prostrate juniper (*Juniperus horizontalis*)
Seaside daisy (*Erigeron karvinskianus*)
Treasure flower (*Gazania* sp.)

Climbers

Bougainvillea sp.
Canary Island ivy (*Hedera canariensis*)
Flame vine (*Pyrostegia venusta*)
Golden trumpet vine (*Allamanda cathartica*)

Plants for tropical and subtropical climates

Plants for these climates need to be able to cope with warm, humid and often rainy summers. The tropical climate is a more extreme version of the subtropical one. Some of the plants below are suitable for either a subtropical or a tropical climate; some are suitable for both. To figure out which is which, use the key below.

S = Subtropical
T = Tropical
ST = Subtropical and tropical

Trees

Australian frangipani (*Hymenosporum flavum*) ST
Bauhinia purpurea ST
Cape chestnut (*Calodendron capense*) S
Cape honeysuckle (*Tecomaria capensis*) ST
Dracaena sp. ST
Firewheel tree (*Stenocarpus sinuatus*) ST
Frangipani (*Plumeria* sp.) ST
Hills fig (*Ficus microcarpa* var. *hilli*) ST
Illawarra flame tree (*Brachychiton acerifolius*) S
Jacaranda (*Jacaranda mimosifolia*) S
Lillypilly (*Acmena* sp.) S
Lillypilly (*Syzygium* sp.) ST
Ponytail palm (*Beaucarnea recurvata*) ST
Royal poinciana (*Delonix regia*) T
Silver cassia (*Senna artemisioides*) T
Umbrella tree (*Schefflera* sp.) ST
Weeping fig (*Ficus benjamina*) ST

Shrubs

Forest flame (*Ixora coccinea*) ST
Oleander (*Nerium oleander*) S
Persian shield (*Strobilanthes gossypinus*) S
Red bauhinia (*Bauhinia galpinii*) ST
Sky flower (*Duranta repens*) ST
Strobilanthes anisophyllus S

Perennials and grasses

Bird of paradise (*Strelitzia reginae*) ST
Dietes iridioides S
Fruit salad plant (*Monsteria deliciosa*) ST

New Zealand flax (*Phormium tenax*) ST
Oyster plant (*Acanthus mollis*) S
Philodendron selloum ST
Philodendron 'Xanadu' ST
Swamp lily (*Crinum pedunculatum*) ST

Annuals

Bachelor's buttons (*Gomphrena globosa*) ST
Brachycome multifida S
Cosmos (*Cosmos bipinnatus*) ST
Ornamental sages (*Salvia* sp.) S
Pigface (*Portulaca grandiflora*) S
Pyrethrum daisy (*Chrysanthemum cinerariaefolium*) S
Spider flower (*Cleome hassleriana*) ST
Sweet Alice (*Lobularia maritima*) S
Verbena (*Verbena* x *hybrida*) S
Virginia stock (*Matthiola maritima*) S

Groundcovers

Alternanthera sp. ST
Bergenia cordata S
Bromeliad sp. ST
Clivia sp. S
Trailing lantana (*Lantana montevidensis*) ST
Wax plant (*Hoya* sp.) ST

Climbers

Bengal clock vine (*Thunbergia grandiflora*) S
Bougainvillea cultivars ST
Bower of beauty (*Pandorea jasminoides*) S
Carolina jasmine (*Gelsemium sempervirens*) S
Coral vine (*Antigonon* sp.) ST
Guinea gold vine (*Hibbertia scandens*) S
Madagascar jasmine (*Stephanotis floribunda*) ST
Potato vine (*Solanum jasminoides*) S
Star jasmine (*Trachelospermum jasminoides*) ST

OPPOSITE, CLOCKWISE FROM TOP LEFT *Syzygium* sp., *Brachychiton acerifolius*, *Plumeria* sp., *Bauhinia gulpinii* and *Verbena* sp.

THIS PAGE, CLOCKWISE FROM TOP *Salvia nemerosa* 'Ostfriesland', *Brachycome multifida*, *Solanum jasminoides* and *Bromeliad neoregelia*.

Plants for a cool temperate climate

These plants experience definite seasonal changes. The winters can be very cold while the summers are mild to warm. Rainfall patterns differ considerably throughout this climate type.

Trees

Callery pear (*Pyrus calleryana*)
Cedars (*Cedrus* sp.)
Common ash (*Fraxinus excelsior*)
Crab apple (*Malus floribunda*)
Cypress (*Cuppressus* sp.)
Desert ash (*Fraxinus griffithii*)
Eastern red cedar (*Juniperus virginiana*)
Elm (*Ulmus* sp.)
Golden robinia (*Robinia pseudoacacia* 'Frisia')
Honey locust (*Gleditsia triacanthos*)
Maidenhair tree (*Ginkgo biloba*)
Peppercorn (*Schinus molle* var. *areira*)
Pin oak (*Quercus palustris*)
Plane tree (*Platanus* sp.)
Red oak (*Quercus rubra*)
Snow pear (*Pyrus nivalis*)
Sweet gum (*Liquidambar styraciflua*)

Shrubs

Abelia x *grandiflora*
Barberry (*Berberis* sp.)
Box (*Buxus* sp.)
Buddleja sp.
Cherry laurel (*Prunus laurocerasus*)
Cotoneaster sp.
Cotton lavender (*Santolina* sp.)
Elaeagnus sp.
English lavender (*Lavendula angustifolia*)
Escallonia sp.

CLOCKWISE FROM TOP *Ulmus glabra* 'Lutescens', *Passiflora* sp., *Vinca minor* and *Oenothera* sp.

Firethorn (*Pyracantha* sp.)
Holly (*Ilex* sp.)
Jade plant (*Portulacaria* sp.)
Mahonia sp.
May bush (*Spiraea* sp.)
Mock orange (*Philadelphus* sp.)
Photinia sp.
Portugal laurel (*Prunus lusitanica*)
Red-barked dogwood (*Cornus alba*)
Roses (*Rosa* sp.)
Silk-tassel bush (*Garrya elliptica*)
Spindle tree (*Euonymus* sp.)
Sweet olive (*Osmanthus fragrans*)
Sweet viburnum (*Viburnum tinus*)
Syrian hibiscus (*Hibiscus syriacus*)
Veronica (*Hebe* sp.)
Weigela sp.
Xylosma sp.

Perennials and grasses

Baby's breath (*Gypsophila paniculata*)
Catmint (*Nepeta* sp.)
Coneflower (*Rudbeckia* sp.)
Corsican hellebore (*Helleborus corsicus* syn. *H. argutifolius*)
Feather grass (*Miscanthus sinensis*)
Feather reed grass (*Calamagrostis* x *acutiflora*)
Gay feather (*Liatris spicata*)
Golden marguerite (*Anthemis tinctoria*)
Hollyhock (*Althaea rosea*)
Lenten rose (*Helleborus orientalis*)
Michaelmas daisy (*Aster novi-belgii*)
Perennial cornflower (*Centaurea montana*)
Pincushion flower (*Scabiosa* sp.)
Poa labillardieri
Purple coneflower (*Echinacea purpurea*)
Red valerian (*Centranthus ruber*)
Russian sage (*Perovskia atriplicifolia*)
Ornamental sages (*Salvia* sp.)
Tall bearded iris (*Iris germanica*)
Wormwood (*Artemesia* sp.)
Yarrow (*Achillea millefolium*)

Groundcovers

Candytuft (*Iberis* sp.)
Garden pinks (*Dianthus* sp.)
Greater periwinkle (*Vinca major*)
Heather (*Erica* sp.)
Ivy (*Hedera* sp.)
Lamb's ears (*Stachys byzantina*)
Lesser periwinkle (*Vinca minor*)
Lilly turf (*Liriope* sp.)
Pachysandra sp.
Rock cress (*Aubrieta* x *cultorum*)
Snowtuft (*Arabis caucasica*)
Stonecrop (*Sedum spectabile*)
Sweet violet (*Viola odorata*)

Annuals and biennials

Adonis sp.
Bachelor's buttons (*Gomphrena globosa*)
California poppy (*Eschscholzia californica*)
Cockscomb (*Celosia cristata* syn. *C. argentea*)
Evening primrose (*Oenothera* sp.)
Flanders or field poppy (*Papaver rhoeas*)
Honesty (*Lunaria annua*)
Love-in-a-mist (*Nigella damascena*)
Night-scented tobacco (*Nicotiana sylvestris*)
Opium poppy (*Papaver somniferum*)
Pigface (*Portulaca grandiflora*)
Queen Annes lace (*Ammi majus*)
Toadflax (*Linaria maroccana*)
Virginia stock (*Matthiola maritima*)

Climbers

Boston ivy (*Parthenocissus tricuspidata*)
Climbing roses (*Rosa* sp.)
Grape vine (*Vitis* sp.)
Happy wanderer (*Hardenbergia violacea*)
Honeysuckle (*Lonicera* sp.)
Passion flower (*Passiflora* sp.)
Pink jasmine (*Jasminum polyanthum*)
Sweet pea (*Lathyrus odoratus*)
Wisteria sp.

Index

Page numbers in **bold** print refer to main entries. Page numbers in *italics* refer to photographs

Acknowledgments

Jonathan Garner would like to thank: the beauty, fortitude and understanding of my wife Fiona and two editors extraordinaire, Sarah Baker and Diana Hill — they truly are masters of their craft; my Mum, Jan Garner, for giving me her insight on plants; Australian Institute of Horticulture Inc.; Merrist Wood College, England; Professor Ed Gillman, University of Florida; Ryde School of Horticulture, Australia; and Leslie Saddington FAIH.

The author and publisher would like to thank the following companies for their assistance with this project: Australian Native Landscapes, Terrey Hills NSW; Belrose Nursery, Belrose NSW; Kulgoa Nursery, Terrey Hills NSW; and Watermatic Irrigation, Hornsby NSW.

Photographic credits

All photographs were taken by Joe Filshie except for the following:
Andrea Jones Back cover (second from right), 10–11, 13, 28–29, 31, 54–5, 75, 106, 162–3. **André Martin** 108–9, 123, 154. **Murdoch Books Photo Library** Front cover flap (left), 21, 60, 67, 73 top, 92, 99, 100, 135, 142, 167 R, 192 (bottom row, middle). **Lorna Rose** 59, 70 R, 103, 105 R, 119, 121, 124, 140, 175, 191, 192 (all but top row, middle, and bottom row, middle), 193 (second row, third row and bottom row R), 194, 195 (all but top row R), 196, 197, 198 (all but middle row). **Sue Stubbs** 17 (left), 42, 64, 69, 70 L, 132, 145 L, 182.

The author and publisher would like to thank the following companies and garden owners for allowing photography specially for this book: Australian Native Landscapes (pp 30, 36–7, 56, 72, 73 bottom, 74); Belrose Nursery (pp 82, 86–7, 91, 96, 141, 146–7, 150, 153, 156–9, 166, 167 L, 170–1, 173, 177–9, 187); Les and Diane Brunell, North Curl Curl NSW (pp 49, 137 L); Annie and Richard Campbell, Lindfield NSW (pp 14, 19, 20 L, 22, 24, 25 bottom, 35, 38, 39 L, 40, 44, 46, 48, 58, 104–5, 114–15, 117, 145 R); Amanda and Andrew Clarke, Mosman NSW (pp 139, 143); Bernard Chapman, Lindfield NSW (pp 84, 128–9, 131, 176, 180); Kulgoa Nursery (p 85); Alec Leopold, Wollstonecraft NSW (pp 20 R, 63, 113, 118, 169 bottom, 172, 174); Watermatic Irrigation (p 134); and Ruth and Ted Woodley, Chatswood NSW (pp 32, 61 L, 65–6, 94–5, 137 R, 151, 181, 183, 186).

The publisher would like to thank the following garden owners in Australia and overseas for allowing photography in their gardens: Abbey House Gardens, Wiltshire UK; Sarah Baker, Leichhardt NSW; Bringalbit, Sidonia, VIC; Brisbane Botanic Garden, Mt Coot-tha QLD; Buskers End, Bowral NSW; Mr & Mrs Andrew Cannon, Manildra NSW; Heather Cant, Burrado NSW; CC Cottage, TAS; Chanticleer Garden, Philadelphia, United States; Chelsea Flower Garden, London UK; Jeanette Closs, Kingston TAS; Colourwise Nursery, Glenorie NSW; Daffs Kitchen, Canberra ACT; Eryldene, Gordon NSW; Flagstaff Cottage, Bowral NSW; G & P Hadjielefttheriadis, Adaminaby NSW; Diana Hill, Ashbury NSW; Galapagos Farm, Bruny Island, TAS; Kennerton Green, Mittagong NSW; R & M Klaassn, Carins NSW; Lindfield Park, Mt Irvine NSW; Luberon, Provence, France; Mercure Hotel, Heritage Park, Bowral NSW; Raylee & Gavin Muir, Te Awamutu, New Zealand; Andrew O'Sullivan, East Sydney NSW, designed and constructed the garden on page 121; Mr & Mrs Park, Canberra ACT; S Parker; L Puglisi & P Sumner, Cammeray NSW (Designer: Tony Wilson); G & G Rembel, Dural NSW; Renaissance Herbs, Warnervale NSW; Rose Cottage, Deviot TAS; Dora Scott, Wahroonga NSW; The Lilian Fraser Garden, Pennant Hills NSW; The Wildflower Farm, Somersby NSW; Thompson Brookes, United States; Titoki Point, Taihape, New Zealand; Winterwood, Mt Tomah NSW; Woodlyn Nurseries, Fiveways VIC; and Yarrawin, Leura NSW.

The irrigation diagram on page 144 is by Di Zign.